Jesus Stories

For the Losers

The Lost

&

The Least

**MINUTE STORIES
FOR
SPIRITUAL REFLECTION**

Publications by Andre Papineau

Jesus & the Kingdom of Nobodies
Passages on the Spiritual Journey
Celebrating Life in Liturgy
Breaking Up, Down & Through
Holding One Another; Being Separate Together
Transitions: Thresholds of Spiritual Awakening
Sermons for Sermon Haters
Let Your Light Shine
Jesus On the Mend
Lightly Goes the Good News
Biblical Blues
Breakthrough: Tales of Conversion

Jesus Stories

For the Losers

The Lost

& The Least

by

Andre Papineau

Copyright © 2001 by Andre Papineau, SDS
All rights reserved
including the right of reproduction
in whole or in part in any form
except in the case of brief quotations
used in articles and reviews.
The Scripture quotations contained herein
are from the New Revised Standard Version Bible,
Copyright © 1989 by the Division of Christian Education
of the National Council of Churches of Christ in the U.S.A.,
and are used by permission.
All rights reserved.
Published by Lemieux International, Ltd.
P. O. Box 170134
Milwaukee, Wisconsin 53217-8011

ISBN: 0-9667269-8-7

Library of Congress Cataloging-in-Publication Data

Papineau, Andre, 1937 –
    Jesus stories for the losers, the lost, and the least / Andre
Papineau.
    p.cm.
    Includes bibliographical references (p.).
    ISBN 0-9667269-8-7 (pbk.)
    1. Bible. N. T. Gospels—Liturgical lessons, English.
    2. Bible N.T.
Gospels—Meditations. I. Title

BS2565 .P37 2001
252—dc21

                                                      2001038017

Acknowledgements

I would like to thank Lemieux International, Ltd. for its hard work and many suggestions which have brought this book to completion. In particular I would like to thank William Lemieux whose insights and attention to detail flow throughout the book; Barbara Olive whose technical expertise and intuition added a unique women's perspective; Michael Olive for creating a provocative cover and illustrations; and David Subat who proofed the book and fine-tuned the grammar.

I would also like to thank the many heroes whom I have encountered within and around the church, who through their lives and chosen service, exemplify the teachings and expectations of Jesus addressed in this book.

Last, but not least, I would like to thank the many members of the congregations, seminars, workshops, and other meetings who have heard these stories, reflected on them, and provided feedback. Without all of you this book would not be possible.

CONTENTS

INTRODUCTION 1

HOW TO USE THESE STORIES 8

1 SHEPHERD'S WELCOMING COMMITTEE ... 11
   Reflection 18

2 JESUS THE PRESENT 20
   Reflection 27

3 CRAZY KINGS 29
   Reflection 35

4 MIXED BLESSINGS 37
   Reflection 43

5 RESTLESS 45
   Reflection 50

6 SQUEAKY CLEAN 52
   Reflection 58

7 DIRTY 60
   Reflection 66

8 SHEEP STORY 69
   Reflection 72

9 OPEN INVITATION 74
   Reflection 80

CONTENTS continued

10 TALENTS 82
    Reflection 86

11 DANGEROUS AFFECTIONS 87
    Reflection 94

12 HEALING TOUCH 96
    Reflection 102

13 WELL, WELL, WELL 104
    Reflection 110

14 SHAME 112
    Reflection 118

15 TREE STUMP 120
    Reflection 128

16 SAVING NEED 130
    Reflection 137

17 VILLAGE OF CLEAN LIVING 139
    Reflection 145

18 BROKEN PROMISE 147
    Reflection 153

19 FIRED UP WITH THE GOOD NEWS 156
    Reflection 162

    EPILOGUE 164

⇛ INTRODUCTION ⇚

Mark 8:1-10 In those days when there was again a great crowd without anything to eat, he called his disciples and said to them, "I have compassion for the crowd, because they have been with me now for three days and have nothing to eat. If I send them away hungry to their homes, they will faint on the way—and some of them have come from a great distance." His disciples replied, "How can one feed these people with bread here in the desert?" He asked them, "How many loaves do you have?" They said, "Seven." Then he ordered the crowd to sit down on the ground; and he took the seven loaves, and after giving thanks he broke them and gave them to his disciples to distribute; and they distributed them to the crowd. They had also a few small fish; and after blessing them, he ordered that these too should be distributed. They ate and were filled; and they took up the broken pieces left over, seven baskets full. Now there were about four thousand people; And he sent them away.

Jesus Stories For the Losers, the Lost, and the Least

The stories in this book are about Jesus and how he turned his and our world upside down by his concern for the losers, the lost, and the least. Throughout the gospels these are the people whom Jesus embraces as members of his family. By singling out familiar biblical stories and retelling them with these categories in mind, we can view and recreate the stories from a fresh and surprising perspective.

To understand more clearly how this can occur it will be helpful to reflect on Mark's account of Jesus feeding the multitude in the wilderness.

When we read this gospel passage do we wonder why the folks in the wilderness got excited that day? What impressed them most? What got them singing alleluias and dancing up a storm? Why might they have even wanted to camp out under the stars that night?

The question isn't what excites us when we read this story, or what has fueled preachers for two millennia to sing the divine praises about the event. The question isn't what intrigues us. <u>We</u> would say it's Jesus producing all that bread and fish! For us that's the miracle! Enough bread to feed an army! That's why we'd be excited.

But the real question is what made the crowd excited. Why did they clap their hands, tap their feet, and cry for sheer joy that afternoon? Do we think <u>they</u> were ecstatic because Jesus surprised them with wonder bread and a ton of fish? Not that they weren't happy to fill their empty bellies! The truth is in such a large crowd most of the folks probably weren't even close enough to see Jesus creating so much out of so little.

No, something else got them cheering – something we wouldn't even think of unless we were in that motley mix of nobodies and somebodies all rubbing elbows with one another. Then if it wasn't the meal what was it that probably inspired them to chant all the way home, "We want to come back! We want to come back!"?

Here's a clue. Imagine your church four times its original size. And continue imagining that a couple of thousand folks hear that Jesus is going to preach, and has sent out the word, "Everybody's invited!" No sooner is the word out than people are streaming in from the suburbs, the inner city, the countryside. What a mix of folks they are! Busy bankers, bag ladies with pushcarts, social butterflies and shady ladies, bleary-eyed derelicts, purple spike-haired teens with rings in noses and ears, folks of every color, married couples, divorced and remarried couples, unmarried straight and gay couples, plus a few shapely ladies with very deep voices–very deep voices–a little too deep for shapely ladies! An observer on the scene might think, "Boy, there's a lot of losers and lost souls showing up–the least likely to get through the doors at the Ritz!

Pouring through the open doors, imagine Jesus smiling from ear to ear, greeting them with open arms, but <u>not</u> screening the winners from the losers by demanding that losers mend their ways before entering the church. "You're out! You got dirt on your soul!"

Or, "You're in! You're clean as a whistle!" Why would he be so careless and carefree about who'd enter?

It was because he was delighted that they showed up. Because he loved to throw parties and surround himself with losers, lost souls, and the least loved, those not likely to get ahead in this world.

And imagine that after listening to him for three days (you can preach that long if you're the boss's son), he invites them to break bread with one another – mingling, interacting, communing with him and one another. Think about it! Communion with Jesus – all the losers, the lost, and the least

This description of what might happen if Jesus came to town is a clue concerning what the really big news was the day Jesus came to be with the Jews in the wilderness.

But a clue to what? The wilderness was a place of chaos for the Jews. It was a place where distinctions between winners and losers was meaningless. Make no mistake. Such distinctions did exist within Jesus' society, especially among the religious elite as they too often do today.

Jesus lived in a highly stratified, segregated society governed in large measure by the purity system. People were considered to be pure or clean if they were physically or morally whole, intact, integral. We'll call them the winners. On the other hand they were impure or unclean if they were physically or morally flawed. These we can call the losers, the lost, and the least. If someone had so much as a zitz, much less other physical imperfections–being blind, or lame, that person was a loser. Or if the person was a tax collector like Zacchaeus, or a bastard, a foundling or fatherless, that person would be a loser or lost. And the list went on.

This segregation of the pure from the impure was especially true of the people with whom one ate. Eating with someone considered impure could render someone previously pure, impure. "Eat with your own kind or else!" was the message. Those with whom one ate said a lot about who belonged and who didn't belong, who was on the winning side and who was on the losing side.

Jesus was of a different mind and heart. He was passionate about breaking down barriers between the clean and the unclean, the winners and the losers– especially around the meal table. Imagine who got to know one another during those three days in the wilderness! Merchants and peasants, landowners and sharecroppers, the healthy and the sick, the morally fit and unfit; all were there. Since we don't read of Jesus screening those coming to hear and eat with him, what we imagine likely matches the reality! Everybody was gloriously out of place in this godforsaken, now god-graced space that day, and Jesus reveled in it!

No wonder his enemies accused him of being a drunk and hanging out with the likes of the Jewish Mafia and prostitutes; in short, other losers. His passion for blurring boundaries between the pure and the impure, the whole and the broken is really compassion. He was passionately compassionate!

Yes, passionately compassionate!

What he did was cross boundaries. He brought people together who otherwise would have remained distant and aloof from one another. The only price of admission to his table was that he be the host, the one who embraced, welcomed and included everybody on the dinner list. Jesus' passion was always to include, not exclude. He sought out the lost, the losers, and least in his ministry. Insiders faulted him for loving outsiders. But if this was a fault, it was a supremely glorious fault!

Did he care about repentance? Yes, he did. But like the father in the story of The Prodigal Son, he couldn't restrain himself from welcoming the lost souls of his society. Like the father, he didn't first demand that his son clean up his act before they sat down to eat.

So what are *we* to learn from what excited the crowd that day? It is fairly easy to sing alleluias about Jesus' abilities as a bread smith. But this makes no demands on us. "Look what *he* did!" we say. It is something else to take seriously his message of compassion in liturgy and life. How serious are we? As described earlier, all we need to do is reflect on our own reaction to the scenario of Jesus welcoming everybody into our congregations. What would we do if those doors opened and a young bearded man cried out with joy, "Open the doors! Open the doors! They're coming! They're coming! What are you waiting for?" A good question.

Would our theology, our politics, our biases,

our fears of reprisals lead us to bar the doors rather than open them wide? Would we be so fearful that in our haste to exclude "those" losers we would even have excluded the young bearded man with the inviting smile, passionately crying out, "Open the doors!"?

It should be apparent why the use of the words, "the losers, the lost, and the least", is helpful in viewing biblical passages when the purity system comes into play. Clean-unclean and pure-impure are terms used over and over in the Gospel stories because these terms technically are more accurate in describing divisions within Jesus' society. However, modern readers can more easily identify with the idea of *the losers, the lost, and the least,* because in our society these words are more suggestive of what people today have experienced.

Finally, I am indebted to Robert Farrar Capon who has used the *losing* categories so effectively in The Parables of Grace (cfr. Chapter 4 "Losing As The Mechanism of Grace in The Parables of Grace", 1988, reprinted 1996, Wm. B. Eerdmans Publishing Co. 255 Jefferson Ave. S.E., Grand Rapids, Michigan 49593)

HOW TO USE THESE STORIES

Individuals can reflect on how these stories differently mirror their own reactions towards themselves and others as they encounter what it means to be lost or losers. e.g., Do they feel anger, disgust, despair, compassion, etc., as they encounter them in their daily life? The reflections offer challenges to reconsider more appropriate responses to the lost and losers in our society.

Parish leaders, preachers, small faith sharing groups, as well as high school teen-agers will all find the stories and the reflections following the stories helpful in deepening their appreciation of Jesus' compassion for those treated like outsiders. They will be challenged to reach out to the outsiders in their midst.

<u>Faith sharing groups</u> will be challenged by the stories to see beyond limited horizons of who God is and what God expects of them. Even with the best of intentions small groups can become preoccupied with their own needs and neglect the needs of the larger church community which envisions God as the one who reaches out to all God's children.

<u>Preachers</u> may be stimulated to use the stories in their sermons. The reflections can serve as the direction(s) in which a preacher hopes to move the

congregation in presenting the story. Of course the preacher is free to adapt the stories and present them as he or she feels suits the occasion. Since many of the stories are highly dialogic they can be delivered by two or three persons during the service on special occasions.

<u>Older high school students</u> can relate to these stories because they are about insiders or cliques rejecting those who appear odd or different from the group for any number of reasons, e.g., physical disability, different moral standards, etc. If teen-agers read these stories it would be helpful for teachers to guide discussions through the use of the reflections, especially if these reflections lead the teen-agers to reflect on their own concerns about being rejected. Teens fear being outsiders because the consequences, e.g., loneliness, loss of self-esteem, etc. are so frightening and even destructive, as so recently evidenced in the tragedies at Colombine High School in Colorado and the Metcalf murders of Milwaukee.

What is often overlooked in using stories is the possibility of presenting an <u>evening of storytelling</u> by older teen-agers for an audience or church congregation. Teen-agers who are talented at telling stories or show the potential for doing so can be invited to participate by choosing stories which are humorous or serious. During the course of the evening they can alternate with one person presenting a story having little or no dialogue, and then two or three presenting a story which has enough dialogue for several persons. One of the teen-agers can act as a narrator for the evening by providing a thematic context, e.g., the physically disabled, the morally bankrupt, the foreigners, etc. Storytelling is a very effective way of communicating the gospel message to people who might be disinclined to listen to lectures on spiritual themes but are open to listening to stories.

If the stories are used for children it should be obvious from reading them that not all are suited. Whenever a story is used, the teacher will need to adapt it to the children's' ability to understand the story.

Finally, it seems that however different groups or individuals use the stories, some might find it helpful to begin by reading the entire gospel passage from which the story is taken, since many persons might not be familiar with the passage. The value of reading the gospel passage can be enhanced when individuals are further stimulated to share their own insights on the passage in question. These stories are intended to serve as a catalyst which allow these insights to occur.

⋙ CHAPTER ONE ⋘

SHEPHERDS' WELCOMING COMMITTEE

Luke 2:15-16 When the angels had left them and gone into heaven, the shepherds said to one another, "Let us go now to Bethlehem and see this thing that has taken place, which the Lord has made known to us." So they went with haste and found Mary and Joseph, and the child lying in the manger.

Daily, Ben described what was happening at the cave on the hillside. While they didn't really believe his stories, they believed he was sincere. They knew he was too simple, too naive to deceive them. Besides, they could appreciate tall stories. Like Ben they were shepherds.

Nobody in Bethlehem trusted shepherds. Respectable folks always wrote them off as liars and thieves. They resented the shepherds who sometimes led their flocks to graze on their lands when they weren't looking. Even worse, shepherding was an occupation which the religious leaders considered impure, immoral. So it made sense that the other shepherds listened to Ben's preposterous stories about the hillside cave without questioning their truth or falsity. If no one else respected these shepherds, at least they could respect one another.

"I've seen him! I've seen him! Ben cried as he ran to one of the shepherds who was guiding a wayward sheep back to his flock.

"You saw who?" the shepherd asked as he placed a hand on Ben's shoulder.

"Moses! I saw Moses in the cave."

"And what was Moses doing in the cave?" the shepherd asked matter-of-factly.

"Checking it out!"

"Did Moses tell you why he was checking it out?"

"To make sure it's in tip top shape for the boss," Ben answered.

"Boss? What boss?"

"I dunno. I didn't ask him," Ben answered. "But he wanted to see it cleaned up a bit!"

"And did you clean it up?" the shepherd asked as he tried to humor Ben.

"Yeh! Yeh! I did," Ben answered proudly.

"Good for you Ben!" Then making an attempt to turn Ben's attention to the matter at hand, the shepherd asked, "Ben, why don't you look after these sheep for a while. I need a break!"

"Sure, sure," Ben obliged. Looking after the sheep was minor business compared with what he had already accomplished at the cave.

Two days later Ben ran breathlessly to another shepherd. "I've seen him! I've seen him!'" Ben shouted.

Having heard about Ben's report to the first shepherd, the second asked calmly, "Who did you see?"

"David! King David!"

"King David?" The shepherd was impressed. "My, but you're getting some important visitors at this cave!"

"Yeh! Yeh! He surprised me when he dropped in. He wants to make sure the place is fit for a king."

"Ohhh! A king? We're expecting a king, are we?" The shepherd feigned surprise. "But why a king, Ben? Certainly not our old Herod. He's not what I'd call a stable king," the shepherd winked.

Ben scratched his nose, thought a minute, and answered, "I dunno. I dunno." He had missed the shepherd's pun.

"A strange place for a king to visit—in a cave—wouldn't you say, Ben?"

"I dunno. I dunno," Ben answered.

"So how did you make it fit for a king?" the shepherd continued.

Ben closed his eyes, scratched his head, and thought for a minute as he strove to recall how he had made the cave suitable for a king's visit. " Just covered the food trough with my mantle, I guess," Ben hesitated. "Yeh! With my mantle!"

"Well that ought to cheer up the king when he visits. But a food trough seems like a pretty small throne for a king, wouldn't you say?" the shepherd asked.

"Yeh! Yeh!" Ben puzzled, unaware that his questioner was teasing him.

"But Ben, how about giving me a hand rounding up these sheep. We're going to lose them if we keep going on about your king's royal visit."

"Sure, sure," Ben agreed. He thought rounding up a few sheep was child's play compared with what the Big Shepherds, Moses and David had asked him to do at the cave.

The next day Ben ran to yet another shepherd. "Guess who I've seen?"

Having also heard the other shepherds' stories about Ben's visits, this shepherd thought he'd anticipate who Ben had seen. "King Solomon the Wise, I suppose."

"Yeh! Yeh! Are you smart! It was King Solomon all right!"

Pleased with himself, the shepherd asked, "And what did Solomon want?"

"Oh, just to know if there were enough of us to serve as a welcoming committee."

"A welcoming committee? For what?" The shepherd had briefly forgotten Ben's story why Moses and David had visited the cave.

"For the king! Remember! The king!"

"For the king...oh, of course, for the king, how could I have forgotten!" the shepherd apologized profusely. "And what did you tell him?"

"Who?" Ben asked.

"Solomon! Solomon! What did you tell Solomon?"

"Gee, I dunno. I'm not sure. I guess I told him that I'd find him as many of us as he wanted."

"You did the right thing Ben. I'm sure all of us will want to be on the welcoming committee. Now do you think that you could give me a hand with these sheep? We've got to get them fed."

"Sure! Sure!" Ben answered as he walked alongside the shepherd. But then he halted, raised a hand, and said, "Ohh! Ohh! I forgot to tell you. Solomon wasn't alone. Hark was with him."

"Hark? Who's Hark?" Obviously the shepherd knew Moses, David, and Solomon. But Hark?

"Hark the herald!" Ben answered.

"And who is Hark the herald?"

"An angel!"

"An angel?"

"Yes, an angel!"

The shepherd searched Ben's eyes intently." "And might I ask what the angel, er, Hark wanted?"

"To tell us that he and a few of his friends were flying in for the king's arrival."

Even though the shepherd had heard some pretty tall tales, he found Ben's latest fantasy too much! "Now Ben, you don't mean to tell me that you expect some angels to wing their way here and be part of the welcoming committee."

"I dunno. I'm just telling you what Hark told me. You'd have to ask him about it."

"Oh!" the shepherd sighed. "C'mon Ben, I think we ought to go home. You could use a good hot bath!"

"Yeh! Yeh!" Ben answered.

"Gotta do something about him," the shepherd mumbled as he shook his head and they headed home.

The next night about fifteen shepherds including Ben were tending their sheep in the starlit fields. Spread out, the shepherds were still within hearing distance of one another. Since there was a full moon, they occasionally glimpsed one another's silhouette against the moonlight. It was a very quiet night, punctuated by the bleating of sheep. However, about two hours into the watch the shepherds heard someone shouting, "He's here! He's here!" It was Ben hurrying from one shepherd to another. "We've got to go and see him. I promised we'd be on the welcoming committee."

"Get a hold of yourself!" one of the shepherds cried. The other shepherds muttered, "He's really getting carried away with all his talk about Moses, David, Solomon, and an angel called Hark!" As if they had reached a consensus, they began running after Ben to restrain him. But Ben galloped faster than any of them, and headed directly for the little cave in the side of the hill.

As the shepherds approached the cave they noticed a dim light emanating from it. "Must be a lantern he's set up in there," one of them said.

However, as they entered the cave their eyes widened. In the middle of the cave was a young woman, a man and a small baby. The baby was lying on a shepherd's mantle in a trough. Beaming, Ben cried, "My mantle!" The young couple beckoned the shepherds to come closer, greeted them, thanked them for welcoming them, and spoke as if they had expected them all along. The shepherds were dumbfounded.

"Feel right at home!" they mumbled as they gathered round the baby in the trough. They couldn't recall ever having had anyone spend the night in this cave.

One of the shepherds laughed. "All this talk about Moses, David, Solomon and Hark readying the cave for a king. We've been conned. There's no king here. Just a family as poor as ourselves!" The mother and father laughed too! And the baby gurgled with delight! "Ben, how did you pull this off?"

"Yeh! Yeh!" the other shepherds asked as they looked to Ben for a simple explanation.

"Pull what off?" Ben asked. "I dunno what you mean!" Tears filled his eyes. There was a long silence. Then the shepherds looked at one another as one of them patted Ben on the shoulder. Ben was a simple man. He didn't know what they meant. He had reported what he had seen and heard. It was now up to them to make sense out of what they saw. Slowly they got to their knees, gazed intently at the child in the trough, and silently pondered in their hearts what kind of a king was in their midst that evening.

Shepherd's Welcoming Committee
Reflection

Shepherds weren't considered acceptable among the religious elite of Jesus' society. The shepherd in this story is simple-minded, and while the other shepherds accept him, they never take him or his stories seriously. They humor him as he tells them about the appearances of biblical personalities in a hillside cove where preparations are being made for someone special. But they aren't ready to enter his world, and appreciate his perceptions. He is the least likely person they'd take seriously, and so he is the least among them. Thus, he has two strikes against him. He is a shepherd and too simple minded to reveal anything worthwhile.

We too might react as the shepherds did to stories coming from persons who seem naive, the least likely to speak credibly how God enters their lives. We interpret their stories critically, maybe even sympathetically, but never appreciating them from their perspective.

If we are resistant to listening to others' stories how God has visited them because their stories don't seem theologically accurate or politically correct, we might be missing God's revelation to them because of our inability to enter into their world and the manner in which they receive God's self revelation. But God enters the world according to the abilities or disposition of the one receiving God. Because we find it difficult to receive God as others do is no reason for concluding God hasn't entered their world.

⇛ CHAPTER TWO ⇚

JESUS THE PRESENT

Luke 2:6-7 While they were there, the time came for her to deliver her child. And she gave birth to her firstborn son and wrapped him in bands of cloth, and laid him in a manger, because there was no place for them in the inn.

Christmas is the day we celebrate Jesus the present. He doesn't need to bring presents. He is our present. When he arrived on the scene years and years ago he didn't come wrapped in fancy colored paper with a big ribbon. Oh no! He came unwrapped. His mom and dad were pleased as punch! They wanted everyone to share their joy. Why?

Not because he won a baby contest. Not because he was a whiz kid. Not because he was a Gerber baby. Oh no! They just loved having a present that cooed and gurgled and dribbled and burped and squirmed...and, oh yes, sometimes pooped! That's what they loved about him.

The news got out to the neighbor kids that Jesus the present had rolled into town. From everywhere they hopped, skipped, and ran to the place where Jesus, Mary, and Joseph, and a stableful of animals were. They could hardly wait to see Jesus as they tumbled in. Then they tickled his toes, counted his fingers, and held each other's hands as they danced around his crib. The questions came flying right and left for Mary.

"Does he leak very much?"

"Did he get here on the donkey express?"

"Can he eat tootsie rolls?"

"Can he play King of the hill with us tomorrow when he grows up?"

"I've got a little brother, too. Boy, does he stink! I hold my nose when I'm around him!"

"I like girl babies. If you had a girl baby, would you call her Jessica?"

They all giggled and tickled Jesus' toes some more. But they got the biggest kick when Jesus cooed, gurgled, dribbled, burped, and squirmed....and, oh yes, sometimes pooped!

The news got out to the folks in the hills. Then the hillbilly shepherds hurried over to greet him and offer him some shepherd pie. They went ga-ga over him! "Golly gee whiz, but he's so tiny," one of the shepherds marveled. "He's got tiny, tiny fingers and tiny, tiny toes and tiny, tiny, eyes and a tiny, tiny nose and a tiny, tiny..."

"Shhh!" a second shepherd jabbed him in the ribs.

"He's just so tiny," the first shepherd muttered sheepishly.

And the space cadets, the flying angels, feathers fluttering and wearing party hats, were beside themselves as they swooshed in from the clouds. "Divine, simply divine," one of them crooned.

"Heaven, I'm in heaven," a second joined in.

"And don't forget, he's our boy!" another angel trumpeted as he passed out cigars.

Then some of them tooted their horns to the heavens as others clapped their hands, tapped their feet, rocked back and forth, and belted out, "Glory, glory, glory...Jesus our present is here." And why did they love him so? Just because he'd coo, gurgle, dribble, squirm, and burp...and, oh yes, sometimes poop!

And oh, did the sheep like him too! They'd flash a sheepish grin, and go ba-ba-ba-ba every time Jesus went ma-ma-ma-ma. Nor could the spotted cows contain themselves. Their udders swinging back and forth, they'd go moo-moo-moo whenever Jesus would coo-coo-coo. Even the old hens, cooped up so long with nothing to do, were clucking like crazy, popping out eggs so fast and furious that they piled up a mile high beneath the hens. And why did they love him so? Just because he'd coo, gurgle, dribble, squirm, and burp...and, oh yes, sometimes poop!

Now the news went out to other countries far, far away. Kings showed up at the stable door.

"Oh mon dieu!" the French king cried. "Magnifique! Fantastique! Gabardique! Regardez l'enfant! Vive le roi! Long live the king!"

"Ein wunderkind!" the German king chortled. "Such a little dumpling mit rosey cheeks und a putton for a schnazz! I chust luf him to death! I'd gif der kit und kaboodle for eine Kind vat looks like him!"

"I can tell you right now, he's going places! You just wait and see," the Burger King nodded.

"Hey man, this is cool! I ain't never seen a pad like this before," the African king chuckled as he brushed up against one of the sheep. "Never thought the What's Happening Brother would hang out in a petting zoo! What d'ya say Frenchy? Life's full of surprises!"

Meanwhile the news also got out to some sad folks hiding out in dark, abandoned warehouses outside of town. Holding onto one another as tightly as possible, they began their journey to the stable. They wore long hooded cloaks covering them from top to bottom so others wouldn't see the ugly scars on their heads and bodies. But every now and then the wind blew the cover of their cloaks, and exposed ugly patches of ashen, white skin. Fearful as they were of being seen in daylight, they had heard something special had happened at the stable. They were determined to get as close to it as possible without drawing attention to themselves. Finally arriving near the stable, they crept cautiously to the stable window. Peering through the window, they stood motionless until a young woman spied them and motioned them to come in. They were stunned.

They had always been told they weren't wanted anywhere, but now this woman invited them to come inside. Didn't she realize who they were? Could anyone want to get close to them? What should they do? As they huddled in a small circle and debated among themselves what to do, their words were drowned out by a commotion within the stable. Curiosity got the better of them. Ever so slowly they opened the stable door. Wow! What a sight! For sore eyes and sore souls!

Directly in front of them a multi-colored circus of people, animals, and angels encircled the young man and woman, and their baby in the manger. What a party! There were party-hatted hens cackling, cows mooing, sheep bah-ing, sequined angels tooting trumpets, shepherds fingering flutes, and kids shrieking with delight. Without noticing it, the hooded strangers began tapping feet and clapping hands to the beat of the music. They hadn't been standing there more than a couple of minutes before the hens stopped cackling, the cows mooing, the sheep bah-ing, the angels tooting, the kids shrieking, and the shepherds fluting. All of them stared at the cloaked figures.

The strangers froze, expecting to be told to leave. But no! All they heard was Jesus cooing, gurgling, dribbling, and burping. Everyone in the circle turned their attention to the baby in the manger. Smiling, the young woman walked over to the strangers and led them to the manger. Now we all know how little babies can put anyone at ease when they're gurgling, cooing, dribbling, and burping. Jesus was no exception. "What a present," the strangers muttered as they bent low to admire Jesus. At that moment Jesus reached up and touched their scarred faces. "Ohhh!" they sighed as their hoods and cloaks fell to the ground. No one had touched them in years! For the first time they felt that they belonged somewhere. No wonder that they fell in love with Jesus! Just for cooing, gurgling, dribbling, squirming, and burping and...for touching their minds and hearts as they had never been touched before.

Everyone one was silent for a moment. Then

the silence was broken by the sound of an egg dropping, then another, and another as one of the hens began cackling in thanksgiving for what was happening that day. Within seconds the celebration was in full swing again as the circle grew bigger. For now not only were the hens cackling, the cows mooing, the sheep bah-ing, the angels tooting, the kids shrieking, and the shepherds fluting, but the strangers had hobbled into the circle as one of the angels named "Hark the Herald" led them in songs of praise for Jesus the present. Yes, Jesus was everyone's present because they realized that it was this little baby cooing, gurgling, dribbling, and burping who had brought everyone together to sing and dance in glad celebration. What greater present could they have asked for that day?

Jesus The Present
Reflection

The story of Jesus begins in the manger where we get a preview of what he will do as an adult as he touches the lepers who visit him. Those who have been excluded from the community's life cannot imagine anyone wanting to have anything to do with them until they are touched by the infant Jesus. But it isn't only the lepers who are welcomed. So, too, are the shepherds. Like the lepers they are losers who live on the boundaries of their society. As for the kings, it doesn't matter that they are royalty. They are gentiles and foreigners. Because of this they are unimportant, the least, compared with the sons and daughters of Abraham.

To the religious elite it wouldn't have mattered whether shepherds, lepers or kings showed up. All were considered unclean, and therefore unwelcome. The only acceptable participants at Jesus' birth would have been the animals and the angels.

The party was a party of losers, the lost, and the least. In this sense the party prefigured those who would be citizens of the Kingdom Jesus preached about. That day on the hillside was remarkable because it was they, not the great, who gathered around the manger to dance in the presence of Jesus. It was also fitting since Jesus was a defenseless child having no rights in his society, and therefore was among its least significant members.

That night the angels rejoiced as a new social order was about to begin.

❯❯❯ CHAPTER THREE ❮❮❮

CRAZY KINGS

Matthew 2:9 – 11 When they had heard the king, they set out; and there, ahead of them, went the star that they had seen at its rising, until it stopped over the place where the child was. When they saw that the star had stopped, they were overwhelmed with joy. On entering the house, they saw the child with Mary his mother; and they knelt down and paid him homage.

They were following a star. Imagine that! Crazy kings following a star. Have you ever dropped what you were doing—reading a novel, working at a computer—to follow a star? Have you ever glanced through your window at the stars, singled one out, and thought, "Gee, I think I'm gonna follow that star!"

No, I don't think so. Nor would I. We'd have to be a little crazy to do something like that.

The story of the three kings is really a story about three crazy people who decided to follow a star. Before they had even met on a lonely stretch of desert, these kings were considered crazy in their own kingdoms. At least this was the consensus of the officials who conducted the kingdom's *serious* business.

One of the kings, dressed in designer clothes, often strolled in one of the poorer neighborhoods near the palace. On one occasion, he spied an old man wearing tattered clothes and shoes. Admiring the old man's attire, the king remarked, "Sir, what a marvelous outfit you're wearing! It's a Brooks Brothers, isn't it?" Startled, the old man thought the king was mocking him, but seeing he was serious, mumbled, "Sure, sure! Why not? It sure beats my ensemble!" Immediately, in the presence of about a hundred of his subjects the king stripped to his underwear, invited the old man to do likewise, and then they exchanged clothes. Elated on wearing the tattered apparel, the king thanked the old man profusely, smiled broadly, and sporting the deal of his life, paraded proudly back to his palace.

If this king's actions seemed strange, it wasn't any stranger than what the second king did daily. Each afternoon he chatted with folks in the local asylum. He'd invite himself over for tea and cookies. Since he visited each patient, he'd enter a room, pour himself and the patient an imaginary cup of tea, and munch imaginary cookies. Then king and patient conversed about the quality of the tea, what they liked or disliked about the cookies, and what the crazy people <u>outside</u> the asylum were up to. After twenty minutes or so of visiting one patient, the king would enter the next room and do exactly what he had done with the previous patient.

By afternoon's end the king confessed to the astonished guard that his bladder was full, and he had eaten way too many cookies! He highly recommended the guard try the cookies himself. He also asked the royal guard request the inmate to give the recipe to the royal chef. One of the newer guards broke into tears since he had mistaken the king for an inmate, and started to straitjacket him until the king's advisor whispered to the guard whom he was straitjacketing.

But the third king seemed crazier than all the others when he fired the entire royal cabinet for spending time designing elaborate weapons of war. Observing how wildly they described the latest weapons, he decided to open the asylums and invite inmates who tended the flower and vegetable gardens to his new cabinet. Then he instructed his previous cabinet to consider residing in the asylum indefinitely so they might learn the art of growing flowers and vegetables for the subjects of the realm.

"Flowers and vegetables?" they asked incredulously. "Instead of playing war games? What a screwy Louie!" they chanted marching arm in arm off to the asylum.

Yes, these kings appeared to be daffy, but mostly to the subjects who thought their kings' behavior totally at odds with the duties of reasonable kings; like getting steamed up at enemies and waging war. But to those folks who benefited from the kings' erratic behavior, all agreed it was better having a daffy king than a dangerous one!

It came as no surprise to any of the subjects the day each king looked up into the starry skies, singled out one, and decided to follow that one star. Since their royal queens and officials never understood their kings' odd behavior anyway, they never bothered inquiring why the kings decided to follow a star, especially this star of all stars. Needless to say, the entire court breathed a sigh of relief that the kings would be traveling abroad for an indefinite period. They had complained among themselves that if their king did not take leave of the kingdom, then they would end up being as cuckoo as the kings!

As the kings set out on their journey, little did they realize they would meet one another on a desert far, far away from their kingdoms. Being the kings they were, it came as no surprise that when they converged, immediately they struck up a conversation and became friends. As they shared their insights on governing their kingdoms, they realized they had much in common. They deeply appreciated hearing one another's stories and unique approach to governing. None of them had ever gotten such high approval ratings at home as they gave one another that night. Even the star seemed to shine more brightly as they began to follow it together.

They had no idea where the star was leading them. But since they enjoyed one another's company, they were unconcerned how much longer they might be traveling.

Eventually the star appeared to stop on the outskirts of a small village named Bethlehem. "Why here?" they wondered. There weren't any houses in sight—only a stable filled with animals. All they heard were sheep bleating, cows mooing, and a baby cooing.

One of the kings motioned the others to follow him into the stable. Inside they found a family of three, the mother, father, and a newborn baby. Surprised, the kings shrugged their shoulders and wondered why the star had led them to this stable filled with animals and a family of three. But their wonder did not prevent them from instinctively doing the kind of things they would have done in their own kingdoms. Thus, one of the kings got on hands and knees, and made funny faces and noises before the baby. The baby cooed and gurgled with delight. And the king who often drank imaginary tea, and munched on imaginary cookies at the asylum offered an imaginary gift to the mother. He called it frankincense and asked if she didn't think it had a distinctive fragrance. The mother's eyes lighted up as she marveled that she had never smelled anything like it before. Not to be outdone by this king's gift, the other kings opened empty hands and offered myrrh and gold. The woman graciously accepted what wasn't there, showed them proudly to her husband, and placed them next to her infant's crib.

Then the kings took the hands of the young woman and man, and danced the Macarena in a circle around the infant. Of course it was no big deal for them to recognize something special, since they had often seen something special in the ordinary folks back home—something that their *saner* officials had never seen. All three of the kings rose to their knees and proudly proclaimed, "This is one special kid!" Having paid tribute, they stood, bowed to their hosts, and began the journey home. They had followed the star to Bethlehem, but the truth is they had always been following a star and they were simply continuing the star-studded journey they had always been on—with the realization that the star was as much on earth that night as it was in the heavens. Crazy, hey?

Crazy Kings
Reflection

Crazy? These kings had an unusual approach to governing their kingdoms, and their style of governing seemed crazy to the "sane" ministers of their kingdoms. This caused the ministers to think the kings unfit to govern.

But the kings were wise and compassionate in dealing with their subjects. They viewed their subjects with dignity and treated them as if they were kings and queens. So the losers and the lost souls the kings governed felt differently about the kings than did their ministers.

Contrary to the advice of his ministers, one of the kings preferred cultivating peace rather than war. We associate winners with those who triumph in battle. We do not relish being seen as weak or soft if it means compromise of any kind. This king could easily be seen as a loser because of his unwillingness to spend time discussing war games.

Approaching the manger the kings appreciated what the ministers would not have understood, namely, that governing wisely is not best served in the interests of war but in welcoming a child who would one day foster peace and compassion as the kings had done in their kingdoms. Couldn't we benefit with a few more leaders who were as crazy as these kings?

CHAPTER FOUR

MIXED BLESSINGS

> **Luke 2:25-26** Now there was a man in Jerusalem whose name was Simeon; this man was righteous and devout, looking forward to the consolation of Israel, and the Holy Spirit rested on him. It had been revealed to him by the Holy Spirit that he would not see death before he had seen the Lord's Messiah.

Mary and Joseph had mixed feelings about the ritual prescribed in law by which Jesus was formally presented to the Lord. Still, they had traveled to Jerusalem on this particular day because they expected Simeon to perform the ceremony. Simeon had a reputation as a devout person. So Joseph and Mary wanted to bring Jesus to the Temple on a day when Simeon was scheduled to be there.

However, when they arrived they found that

for some reason Simeon wasn't there. Mary and Joseph were disappointed, but soon they were relieved when they found another elder was present who could perform the ritual. "I'll always remember today," Mary sighed when it was over.

"Yes," Joseph said. "We've been blessed, and now we can be on our way. It's too bad Simeon wasn't here, but it all went well anyway." Gathering their belongings, they began walking toward the huge doors which opened to the Temple courtyard.

"Wait! Wait!" someone cried. Jesus and Mary turned to see an old man waving a hand and leaning on a cane with the other. Hobbling along, he apologized, "I'm so sorry, I...oh, let me catch my breath!" Slightly stooped, judging from his flowing, snow white hair and long beard, he had to be about eighty. Catching his breath, he continued, "I've looked forward to this day for years, and wouldn't you know? I took a nap and overslept in my study. I was so upset I almost cried. Then I thought, "maybe, just maybe, I'd still have a chance to see your son."

"Are we supposed to know you?" Mary asked. Something about him was upsetting.

"Oh forgive me! My name is Simeon. I was scheduled to perform the ceremony today."

"Oh, you're Simeon." A sense of relief filled her face. "Well, we hoped you would be here. So we were disappointed when we were told someone else was taking your place. But did I hear you right? That you were looking forward to this for years?"

"Oh, you heard me alright. I was determined to see this day before I breathed my last breath."

Mary was mystified. What did he mean? He looked forward to this day for years? A year ago she didn't even know she'd have a child, or that her family would be here in the Temple.

Simeon seemed not to notice the question on her face. "And I'll tell you, your boy has quite a future ahead of him," he continued, stroking his beard.

More curious than ever, Mary asked, "Would you mind sharing what you know about his future?"

"By all means! By all means!" Simeon answered, winking at Jesus cuddled in Mary's arms. But he was in no rush to tell them. Instead he patted Jesus' head, tickled his feet, and made funny faces. Jesus gurgled and tugged away at his beard. "Such a cute baby you are. Yes, yes, such a nice baby."

Mary and Joseph beamed. "Isn't he a sweet old man?" she whispered to Joseph.

"Yeh! He'd make a great grandpa!" Joseph answered.

"Yep! You're a sweet, little baby. Who'd ever think what a real troublemaker you're gonna be when you grow up?" Simeon laughed as the baby continued tugging his beard.

"Troublemaker?" Now Mary and Joseph laughed. "You've got a great sense of humor," Mary said. "Jesus? A troublemaker? Not our Jesus," she said, kissing his fingers.

Simeon chuckled. "Oh, wait and see! Even before he's thirteen, you'll both be getting a full blown panic attack when the three of you come back here. Your son will take off on his own for a couple of days. My advice is bring along some schnapps! It'll calm

your nerves. You'll need it. But don't worry! He'll be okay. He'll be teaching the elders here a lesson or two before they rest in old Abraham's bosom."
Raising a finger, he continued, "Oh...before I forget, there's one more thing about this trip! Don't be upset if he tells you he's got more important business than hanging around with you folks. Now don't take it personally. Oh no! He won't be mouthing off, just telling the truth."

After listening to Simeon, Mary and Joseph could easily have used the schnapps Simeon had recommended. They hadn't expected to hear his troubling words, not from a holy man their neighbors praised so highly.

Mary decided she had heard enough about her son's future. She nudged Joseph, "I guess it's time for us to go."

"Yeh! Right! We oughtta be on our way." They began inching their way toward the door, but Simeon wasn't finished.

"Oh no! Don't go! Not yet!" Simeon pleaded, waving a hand in the air. But once more he was charmed by the child whose future he was so blithely predicting. "Cootschy, Cootschy, Cootschy Coo." Again Simeon made funny faces. Jesus gurgled, cooed, smiled, and kicked his feet in the air. Simeon was in a playful mood, and for a moment this seemed more important than talking about Jesus' future. Mary and Joseph were relieved. They had already heard enough, and they preferred that Simeon keep any new disclosures to himself. But Simeon couldn't be stopped.

His playful mood at an end, he continued, "Oh yes, when Jesus is thirty and has left home, don't be surprised if occasionally he ignores you when you visit him. Or that he'll be preaching to others to resist their folks who'd block them from following him."

Mary bit her lip. Out of respect, she withheld telling him he must be feeble minded. How could her son even think of leaving his family? No parents' sons left their families. If they did, it was as if a death had occurred since family connections were often severed when a son or daughter left home. And it was unthinkable that her son would think of telling others to follow in his footsteps if their folks prevented them from joining him. It didn't make sense. "Joseph we've got to go. I'm upset, really upset!"

"I am too Mary," he answered.

"We have to leave now," Mary said as she and Joseph abruptly began walking towards the door.

"Wait!" Simeon said. Mary and Joseph halted. When they turned and looked at him his demeanor had changed. Leaning heavily with both hands on his cane, he looked sad. "I shouldn't have spoken so lightly. I didn't mean to offend you. I know you're anxious to leave. But just a few more words? Please?"

Mary and Joseph hesitated, but then slowly walked over to Simeon. "Yes. What do you want to tell us?"

Simeon looked intently into Mary's eyes. "A time will come when you will think your son is not in his right mind and you will want to lock him up because of his preaching."

"Never!" Mary sighed. "Never!"

"Oh yes," Simeon insisted. Mary's eyes filled with tears. How could this man whom she had never met say all these things about her son? "Let me add," he continued, "whatever I've said doesn't mean your son is going to be a rebel, and nothing more. Far from it! Let me put it another way!" Extending both hands to Jesus, he asked Mary, "May I?" At first she hesitated, but then handed Jesus to him.

His face glowed as he looked at the infant's eyes. Praising God, he said, "Master, now you are dismissing your servant in peace, according to your word; for my eyes have seen your salvation, which you have prepared in the presence of all peoples, a light for revelation to the Gentiles and for glory to your people Israel." Both Mary and Joseph were amazed at what Simeon was saying about their son. Then Simeon handed Jesus back to Mary and added, "This child is destined for the falling and the rising of many in Israel, and to be a sign that will be opposed so that the inner thoughts of many will be revealed..." and then Simeon choked up as tears flowed from his eyes. Then he added softly, "and a sword will pierce your own soul too."

Mary didn't know what he meant, and she was afraid to ask. Yet he had given her and Joseph enough to ponder on the journey home. Simeon said nothing more. He simply turned and walked away. Yes, she thought, he had given them much to think about. And as the years rolled by she would sadly discover just how accurate he was about the sword that would pierce her heart. This day had been a day of mixed blessings.

Mixed Blessings
Reflection

Imagine if Simeon had clearly known what Jesus' life would be like as described in Mixed Blessings! A twelve year old who appears indifferent to his parents' feelings (Luke 2:41-51), then becomes a man who leaves his family, and urges others to leave their families if they stand in the way of following him (Matthew 10:34-38). How would Mary and Joseph have reacted if Simeon had told them that Jesus would refuse to speak to his family, and that they'd seriously consider restraining him because they'd think he was unbalanced? (Mark 3:20-35)

Then Simeon's description could have been interpreted as that of one who was lost since Jesus didn't conform to what was normative for a pious Jew within family and community. The truth is if Simeon had actually predicted what is described in Mixed Blessings, he would have accurately reflected what we read about Jesus in the gospels.

To what extent does our compassion compel us to transcend the interests, biases, and preferences of our biological families in favor of the larger human family as it did in Jesus' life? Couldn't we expect to experience some conflict if those interests collided with the needs of this larger family to which we all belong? If so, wouldn't those close to us think we had lost our way because we were in conflict with what they considered normative?

≫ CHAPTER FIVE ≪

RESTLESS

Mark 1:9-11 In those days Jesus came from Nazareth of Galilee and was baptized by John in the Jordan.

Luke 12:49-50 "I came to bring fire to the earth, and how I wish it were already kindled! I have a baptism with which to be baptized and what stress I am under until it is completed!"

Two of Jesus' friends were engaged in conversation as they walked down the main road of Nazareth.
"Today's the day Jesus is thirty," his friend announced.
"And he's as restless as ever," the other added.
"But everything's going his way", the first

puzzled.

"Maybe so. But still he's restless," the second insisted.

"Over what? For what? Is it money he wants?"

"Never talks about money."

"Could he be after a woman?"

"Oh, Jesus admires them but he doesn't seem to want one."

"Power maybe?"

"He laughs at it!"

"Maybe he needs religion?"

"Religion? Ha! I'm not so sure. Says he gets no consolation from laws that bind, or man's mindless rituals. And he can't stomach pious clergy deciding the fate of folks by dictating the last jot and tittle of walking here or there, and eating this or that. In short, he seems to detest religions that clutter, overwhelm and destroy folks."

Jesus' friends weren't the only ones talking either. Certainly none of the neighbors knew.

"He's been rubbing the soreness out of my back since he was a boy," old Mrs. Klinski recalled. "Never grumbled a bit. Can't figure why he'd be restless."

"Same here," shrugged Mr. Liebowitz. "I love his stories. Real whoppers they are! Keeps my spirits up when he's around.".

"When I'm feeling lonely who pops up but Jesus, carrying a big six pack of Jericho Lite," grinned blind Mr. Goldberg, rapping his cane on the porch. "I figure the two of us keep Jericho beer in business. That Jesus is some fellow. Got no reason to be restless. Everyone likes him. He likes everyone. Simple as that!"

Yes, he liked everyone and they all liked him as far back as anyone could remember. But by age thirty, a change had taken hold in him. He told his mother, "I'm restless. I pace the floor and stare out the window. I keep wondering what I've got to find. I'm thirsty and I don't know why. All I know is I gotta leave Nazareth town."

She only smiled and said nothing.

It was not long before Jesus was saying his good-byes, and waving a hand to all the folks he loved. At thirty Jesus left Nazareth town with nothing more than a knapsack strapped to his back.

"Why so restless?" the townsfolk wondered as they sadly watched him disappear down the long winding road.

Wandering days on end, Jesus found himself standing on Jordan's banks. He wasn't alone. Men, women, and children lined the mudbrown banks, waiting their turn to be plunged into the river by a solitary figure clothed in camel skins. Pointing to him, Jesus asked a stranger, "Who is he?"

Surprised Jesus didn't know the center of everyone's attention, the stranger answered, "The Baptizer. John's his name."

"John?" Jesus strained to identify the figure in the sunlit water. "Yes,...yes of course." He recognized his cousin whom he hadn't seen for years. He remembered when John left Nazareth. Everyone said,

"He can't settle down. He's restless—maybe even mad!" No one had understood why John was restless either. In fact the last anyone heard, John had disappeared into the wilderness.

"But what's he doing here?" Jesus asked himself aloud.

"Challenging us to change our lives because God's reign is on the horizon. In other words, he's telling us we can't stay standing still. He says, "Things have gotta change. What we need is a change of heart," said a man standing next to him.

The man's words triggered something in Jesus."God's reign ...we can't stay standing still...things have to change." Mulling the words over in his mind, Jesus stood motionless for several minutes.

"That's it!" he whispered. "God's reign...God's reign...God's reign..." Then lifting his eyes towards the billowing clouds he continued, "No wonder my heart's been restless. Now I know why I had to leave Nazareth town. Scanning the horizon, he thought, "I've come to start a fire on this earth–how I wish it were blazing right now. I've come to change everything right-side up–how I long for it to be finished."*

Finally, readjusting his sight on the long undulating line of people wading into the waters towards John, Jesus made his decision. He too wanted to be baptized because he now understood why he had been so restless. For an hour he stood waist deep in water, waiting his turn. Then he faced the Baptizer who didn't seem at all surprised to see his cousin standing before him.

Looking intently into Jesus' eyes, John smiled and said, "I've been waiting for you. I knew you'd come. The time is at hand for change. You can't stand still. Your heart is ready for more, much more." Without waiting for a response, he placed his rough hands on Jesus' head, and gently lowered him into the water. Emerging from the water, Jesus was consoled by words welling up from within, "You are my beloved; on you my favor rests."

He experienced a peace he hadn't known for months. And the consoling words kept ringing in his ears. "You are my beloved, you are my beloved...." His heart beat faster, and his face was flushed. Tears formed in his eyes. He didn't want to move from the spot but he realized standing still was precisely what he couldn't do, either at Nazareth or here.

Embracing Jesus, the Baptizer confirmed Jesus' intuition by pointing to the desert beyond Jordan's banks. "Go," John said. "You have much to do, and it's time to begin." Jesus was ready. The blaze had been ignited, the fire lit to bring about God's reign. Only later would he realize he had another baptism to undergo, and the anguish he would feel until it was over. Now, however, he was on his way. And once more it wouldn't be long before he was driven into the desert by a restless spirit, God's spirit, to meet the first test as God's beloved.

*The last scriptural quote in this paragraph is Eugene H. Peterson's translation from The Message, Colorado Springs: NAVPRESS 1993, p. 152

Restless
Reflection

What prompted Jesus to leave Nazareth? We have no clue what his life was like prior to his baptism. If he were restless, was it because he wanted to alleviate the burdens which others suffered under the Romans? Or because he desired to do something about a system in which people could easily be categorized as life-time losers? Or was it in response to John's challenge from the banks of the Jordan that people undergo a conversion of heart. Is this why Jesus left Nazareth?

Whatever the reason or reasons Jesus had for leaving his family, it's plausible that he felt restless in Nazareth when he left.

Finally he reached the Jordan and there it happened. As he was baptized he experienced an overwhelming sense of being loved by God. He was God's beloved on whom God's favor rested. This disclosure of God's special love for Jesus revealed that Jesus already rested in the heart of God. Was this a pivotal moment in his life? Certainly, if Jesus' profound awareness of being God's beloved transformed his restlessness into a restless desire to preach God's special love for all who felt alienated from their communities.

We might learn to value our own restlessness if it assists us in experiencing the loss of what had given us a false sense of who we are or what is important in life. Feeling lost, we would then discover the truth about ourselves which St. Augustine discovered when he said, "Our hearts are restless until they rest in thee." Our restlessness is a reminder that ultimately only God can totally satisfy. Such a reminder might also help us be less restless about our losses!

⇛ CHAPTER SIX ⇚

SQUEAKY CLEAN

Mark 7:1-5 Now when the Pharisees and some of the scribes who had come from Jerusalem gathered around him, they noticed that some of his disciples were eating with defiled hands, that is, without washing them. (For the Pharisees, and all the Jews, do not eat unless they thoroughly wash their hands, thus observing the tradition of the elders; and they do not eat anything from the market unless they wash it; and there are also many other traditions that they observe, the washing of cups, pots, and bronze kettles.) So the Pharisees and the scribes asked him, "Why do your disciples not live according to the tradition of the elders, but eat with defiled hands?"

"Clean I say. Clean, clean, clean—that's what we gotta be! After all, cleanliness is next to godliness. And if we want to be acceptable to the Holy One, then we gotta be squeaky clean!"

"Right on! Right on!" Everyone in the room agreed Abe had summed it up beautifully. It was their duty to be squeaky clean each day, especially before meal time. And they agreed that anyone who wasn't clean would be barred from entering the room.

"Fellas we've got to be careful we don't let every Tom, Dick and Harry–not anyone in here who's got the slightest trace of dirt on 'em. And we know who some of those folks are, don't we?"

"Yeh! Yeh! We know! We know!"

"Of course we do." Abe winked at them."There's no room for your run-of-the mill riff raff—like those fellas with the blotchy purple stuff on their skins, or those shady ladies down the block, or those limp wristed twits infiltrating our neighborhoods. I say if we let them in, this will be the dirtiest place in town. And we don't want that now, do we?"

"No! No! No!" the others chanted. The thought of permitting limp wristed neighbors, whores, beggars, and crazies, to name only a few dirties, caused them all to tremble, tremble!

"You know what their presence would do to us, don't you?" Abe whispered ominously. "Contaminate us!"

"Oh! Oh! Oh!" the others groaned, beating their breasts.

"And then the Holy One would be offended

because we'd be dirty just like them."

"Oh! Oh! Oh!" Again the others groaned, while a few fainted and had to be revived.

"So fellas now that we've reviewed our priorities, what do you say we do what we can to insure we're squeaky clean? As you know we always give ourselves a little time to review what we think will be helpful in making ourselves presentable to the Holy One. So let's open the floor for discussion." Abe scanned the elite gathering for some words of wisdom.

At the back of the room one of the guests waved a hand. "I've found Irish Spring to be great for showering up. You feel fresh. You smell fresh. Everybody else tells you how fresh you look, and..."

"Yeh," someone interrupted, "but I've heard the Holy One is turned on by Safeguard. It has a manly scent to it!"

"True," a third added, "but if you're looking for something that'll give you a clean feeling throughout the day try Obsession on the cheeks—all four of them—along with Old Spice under the arms, and Lavoris five times a day to rinse your mouth of any impurities. As a bonus you'll get that added minty taste."

"Now you're crackin! You're on to something!" The others applauded their approval.

Abe raised a finger as he added, "And make sure to keep those bathrooms clean too. Nothing like tidying up with Tidy Bowl—at least that's what that little guy in those Tidy Bowl ads suggests. And he oughtta know since he's spent so much time in the bowl." Abe was pleased that he had given them something to think about which might have gone unnoticed. "But fellas now that we've gotten a few ideas on being squeaky clean so as to be sweet smelling incense rising up to please the Holy One's nose buds, let's get to work. We've got to put on our aprons and make sure we've scrub-a-dub-dubbed our pots and pans and tableware. We did this yesterday, but who knows? Dust might have accumulated since we met, and I'd sure hate to think that everything would be ruined because we hadn't noticed. I mean you don't want to make the Holy One mad or something!"

Without missing a beat the guests removed aprons from plastic bags neatly stacked on a table. Then they donned their aprons and zealously began cleaning the pots, pans and tableware. Everyone was so engrossed in what they were doing that they failed to notice a young man who had entered through a side door. He stood there silently watching as he shook his head in disbelief. Then he coughed to get their attention.

Abe glanced up and froze as his eyes met the eyes of the man. "Jesus!" he whispered. All in the room turned to the intruder and echoed Abe."Jesus!"

"What are you doing here?" Abe demanded.

"I thought you might have room for another dinner guest," Jesus answered.

"But, but, but you're not, not..."

"Not clean. Is that what you wanted to say? Not clean?" Abe mumbled something as Jesus continued.

"No, not by your standards. I was with a few limpwrists, whores, and crazies as you'd call them. So I guess I'm dirty all over."

The guests gasped as they fell back a step or two. "Unclean! Unclean!" they hissed.

Abe came to the defense. "You call down the Holy One's displeasure by your wanton disregard for our tradition. We are called to be clean, clean I say. Cleanliness is next to godliness. No ...cleanliness is godliness!"

"Yeh! Yeh! Give it to him!" the others urged Abe.

Jesus calmy answered, "Yes, my friend, but the Holy One is also the Compassionate One. You've all spent so much time and energy keeping squeaky clean on the outside that you've spent no energy examining whether your tongues and hearts are clean. Where's your compassion for those you write off as unclean? Nowhere as far as I can tell."

"Party pooper!" someone cried.

"Party pooper, you say?" Jesus shot back. "You call this a party? It's just a mutual admiration society. When you open the doors, invite all those you've rejected! Then you'll have a party, the kind the Compassionate One rejoices in." By this time everyone had turned their backs on him. "I see I'm making you sick. Sorry I didn't spic and span myself ahead of time. I guess I'll just have to party with the losers down the street. They're my kind of people anyway. See you fellas!" And Jesus blew them a kiss and walked out the door.

"Well, well," Abe said.

"Well, well," echoed the others.

"Carry on men, and make sure you clean that buffet table Jesus was leaning on." Several of the men rushed to the table with their cleaning fluids. The Holy One would be pleased. Now everything was squeaky clean!

Squeaky Clean
Reflection

In the purity system the desire to be clean is a way of saying "I want to be whole and holy as God is whole and holy." Underlying this desire is the desire to be acceptable to God by doing and maintaining those things which make one clean. There is nothing wrong with wanting to be acceptable to God but the desire to be "squeaky" clean is excessive. It becomes an exercise in which we try to prove ourselves acceptable. If we don't win our way into the heart of God, won't we be losers? How can a loser find himself or herself in God's heart? With this line of thinking, unwittingly we are attempting to manipulate God into loving us.

Today we might find this obsession with being clean a strange way of proving ourselves acceptable to God. But we have our own rituals—secular ones perhaps—but rituals nonetheless in which we try to win others' approval whether through cosmetics, dieting, deodorants, or pushing the right buttons, and saying the right things to impress others. We abhor being a loser. Who wants to hear the words, "Get lost!"

This extends to our relationship with God. Pin

the ten commandments on the wall, or recite a set of prayers, or go to church regularly and we're home safe! God is obliged to give us the stamp of approval. If we think God accepts us because we have done these things, then we aren't any different from the persons who hoped to find approval by being squeaky clean.

It might surprise us to realize, as Paul Tillich has written, that salvation is accepting the fact that we are already accepted by God. What we do after that in response to being accepted ought to be a grateful acknowledgment in word and deed to the God who has accepted us. There's no need to get lathered up about trying to be acceptable! We are already there. Now we can reach out and accept others as God has accepted us.

CHAPTER SEVEN

DIRTY

Mark 4:3-8 Listen! A sower went out to sow. And as he sowed, some seed fell on the path, and the birds came and ate it up. Other seed fell on rocky ground, where it did not have much soil, and it sprang up quickly, since it had no depth of soil. And when the sun rose, it was scorched; and since it had no root, it withered away. Other seed fell among thorns, and the thorns grew up and choked it, and it yielded no grain. Other seed fell into good soil and brought forth grain, growing up and increasing and yielding thirty and sixty and a hundred-fold.

"You're a dirty old man. You always were. You always will be." Accusations came from every direction. Too bad! But Adam could hardly blame people for accusing him of being a dirty old man.

He was a shepherd. Automatically that made him dirty as far as the religious authorities were concerned. In their estimation shepherding was an immoral occupation. Shepherds were known to let their sheep graze on other people's property. They could be crooked. No wonder the staff they used to guide their sheep was called a crook. Adam thought their judgment unfair. "You'd think I was a used cart salesman. But at least no one calls them dirty. Maybe sleazy, but not dirty."

But there was more to this dirt business than being at the bottom of an immoral barrel. Counting sheep in dreamland is one thing; tending them ankle deep in sheep poop, another! Pheww! It's no wonder that even Adam's wife wasn't crazy about his work. Why should she be? Every time he came from work she almost fainted, because he smelled like he had a whole shipload of sheep with him. Of course she couldn't help complaining about the dirt under his nails, on his bib overalls, and the soles of his shoes since she spent hours scrubbing his clothes at the local stream. But what upset her most was when they visited friends. "Adam, whenever we visit the Muskovitzes I want to hide under a chair. It's so bad, Morris and Minnie begin cleaning their rugs and furniture before we've even said goodbye."

Adam sighed. Had it only been about his neighbors holding their noses while passing them on his way to work, or snubbing him because of his work, that would have been depressing enough. But to make matters worse, he had a roving eye for the other shepherds' wives. Not that he had ever tried anything dishonorable. But the other shepherds were especially leery when Adam came within twenty feet of their wives. "What a schmuck" they'd warn their wives. "Watch out for him. He's a dirty old man." Adam knew of his reputation, and he wasn't proud of it. He wasn't sure whether he disliked being known as a dirty man, or an old man, but a dirty old man? That hurt! After all, as a young man he was attractive, and enjoyed hearing others call him a ladies' man. But now... the reputation of being a dirty old man was a death sentence!

    He wondered how he had gotten into this mess. He wanted to blame his great forefather, the first Adam since he was made out of dirt, and the name Adam meant earth-man. But it was a stretch to blame that Adam who lived long ago for his problems. However, Adam thought the religious authorities shared some of the blame. They had condemned him because of his job just as they had condemned the tax collectors. "Oy Vey," he muttered. Placing him in the same category as those turncoat tax collectors was an insult.

    Adam felt far removed from the Holy One who was cleanliness itself. He was taught cleanliness wasn't just close to godliness; it was godliness. Given the Holy One's reputation, Adam imagined himself approaching the Holy One's Kingdom Gates, seeking permission to enter. He pictured Mr. Clean, the big fellow with the golden earring, checking him out from top to bottom, and then angrily shouting, "We don't want dirty old men up here. What do you think we're operating? A hot bed for seedy old men? Go back where you came from? Only the spic and span get through these gates!"

Adam sighed. There wasn't room on earth for dirty old men either. He felt as distant from the Holy One as he could be. Mulling over this one afternoon as he walked on the outskirts of the village, he noticed a small crowd gathered on a hillside. They appeared to be listening intently to a young preacher. Adam felt he might as well go over and listen.

Getting close to the preacher wasn't a problem since the crowd gave him plenty of room when they recognized Adam heading their way. He sat on the ground about ten feet from the preacher. "It's Jesus," he thought. He had seen him only once. That happened when Jesus argued with the same authorities who despised Adam. Wherever Jesus went, he spoke about the Holy One's Kingdom, the Kingdom which seemed so distant from Adam's heart.

Jesus noticed Adam and smiled. Then he began telling a story about seed, and the soil needed for its growth. As Adam listened to Jesus speaking about the kinds of soil which didn't help the seed grow, he noticed Jesus looking at him while he spoke about the best soil that was needed. The best soil? And what was that? Dirty dirt! And what made up dirty dirt? Old fish heads, sheep poop, rotten vegetables and fruit. That's where the Kingdom could take root. "Do you understand?" Jesus asked the crowd. They mumbled among themselves. No one answered.

But Adam's eyes widened. Dirt he understood. Dirt was his name. Dirt was his occupation. Dirt was his temptation. "Yes, yes, I understand!" Adam cried as he hit paydirt!

"Good!" Jesus laughed and clapped his hands. "Everything that everyone else rejects makes up that dirt. God's reign takes root in the dirt, not where everything is clean and tidy, but in the dirt. God's reign happens in the least likely places. Get it?"

Mumbling again, the crowd tried to make sense out of what Jesus told them. But it all made sense to Adam. Grinning from ear to ear, Adam shouted, "It's great news!"

Jesus winked at Adam. "Yes, it's great news because the Kingdom is as close as the dirt under your nails. And since it is, go and tell this news to anyone who'll listen! Go earth man, go!" Adam was dumbfounded. Jesus called him earth man, him, Adam! For the first time he was proud of his name. Jumping to his feet, he embraced Jesus, and bolted through the crowd. "I've found the Kingdom and it's right where I've always been. In the dirt!"

That day Adam was the happiest dirty old man alive!

Dirty
Reflection

Dirt has negative connotations while those associated with clean are positive. If a young man is brought to trial for a heinous crime, his lawyer will advise his client that he appear neat and clean. If he looks like he's lived as a fugitive in the woods, he'll need to be clean shaven and have his hair properly cut. Hoping that being clean will help, the lawyer attempts to impress the jury that his client is innocent. Maybe then, the jury will believe the young man is ready to clean up his act and begin living with a clean slate!

However, those who do the dirty work like washing floors, cleaning public toilets, or sweeping trash in public places might strike some of us as "beneath" the work we do. They're the little people, the folks we seldom notice, or care to notice. We wouldn't demean ourselves by doing dirty work like cleaning public toilets. Do we then think that people who clean bathrooms or wash floors are inferior because they are doing dirty work? If we think them inferior, are we any better than Jesus' contemporaries who might have considered the shepherds dirty or losers because of their occupation?

The difference between being clean and unclean in Jesus' day and ours is more a matter of economics for us. We have a poor underclass, and they are the least in our society. Then we have a middle, and a wealthy upper class. Earning power determines those who are "inferior" or "superior" in spite of our protestations that all are created equal. The man or woman who cleans the toilets in the building is involved in a menial task, earns little, and is treated differently from the man or woman who owns the building.

Whatever classifications we use, the distinction between clean and unclean, who's significant, and who's insignificant is still very much alive. The day we see a CEO fraternizing at home with the man or woman who scrubs the office floors, is a sign that a new reality is emerging where the least among us is given the gracious reception Jesus gave the least in his society.

➤➤ CHAPTER EIGHT ➤➤

SHEEP STORY

Luke 15:4-5 "Which one of you, having a hundred sheep and losing one of them, does not leave the ninety-nine in the wilderness and go after the one that is lost until he finds it? When he has found it, he lays it on his shoulders and rejoices. And when he comes home, he calls together his friends and neighbors, saying to them, ˜Rejoice with me, for I have found my sheep that was lost."

"Dumb! Dumb! Dumb!" is how they described Denny. They were convinced that Denny was the dumbest sheep around. Not that any of them were ready to admit what everyone else knew about them, namely, they were all dumb. And not only dumb but very smelly! But as far as the sheep were concerned, Denny was the dumbest and most smelly one.

"Phewww! Get a whiff of Denny!" they whispered whenever Denny got within sniffing distance. Flocking together, they chanted, "Big dumb Denny stinks! Big dumb Denny stinks!" because he was the biggest sheep in the flock of a hundred. So naturally he'd be the likely one to smell the worst, and the target of the others' attacks. Ears flopping, Denny lumbered all over, sometimes tagging behind the others, but more often off by himself. They taunted him because he was always out of step. "He doesn't think as we think, or act as we act. Nothing is black and white for him as it is for us," they sniffed. "And while we're at it," they giggled, "he's the only black sheep among us. Too bad for Denny."

Forming a chorus line, they danced with the precision of the Rockettes. "We know what's expected of us as we shuffle forward and backward, backward and forward, left to right and right to left! Thank god we're not like Denny! If he weren't so dumb, he'd be lucky to be wooly-minded like us!" Taking their cue from one another, the chorus repeated their dance while chanting, "Big dumb Denny's lost! Big dumb Denny's lost!"

Poor dumb Denny! How did he take it? "Yeh, they're right. I'm not very smart. I don't have all the answers. There are lots of things I'm not clear about. I'm always getting lost, not knowing where I'm supposed to be. And, gee, I do smell horrific! I've used tons of Woolite, and I smell the same. I'm not like them at all." Denny sighed. Shaking his floppy ears he continued, "They do everything together: they rise together, eat together, nap together, play together, poop together, and get fleeced together! They're so lucky! Yeh, I don't fit in. I must be a real loser!"

And how did big dumb Denny feel about all this? "Well, it's not all that bad. I wouldn't have seen all the paths I've seen if I hadn't gotten lost, and I wouldn't have discovered different hills for grazing unless I had been confused. Nor would I have been able to relax, and enjoy the scenery if I had been crowded in with the others. It's been scary, but it's been fun too!"

Yes, Denny was big and dumb but he didn't mind. And every now and then when one of the other sheep, frequently a lamb, strayed from the flock, big, dumb, floppy-eared, smelly Denny was usually close by, ready to soothe the panic stricken sheep because Denny knew the terrors as well as advantages of getting lost.

Of course incidents like this never made the news in the Sheep Gazette because the sheep simply couldn't accept the fact that any of them could be so dumb and lost. As long as they did everything together they felt they simply had to be right. If any of them ever had the slightest suspicion of being lost, it was better not to mention it. After all, they believed they were admired and loved most by their shepherd when they all stayed together, and knew exactly where they were going. Every night before bedtime they'd chant their favorite mantra, "Stay, not stray! Stay, not stray! Stay, not stray!" Then they'd go off to sleep.

And if their mantra didn't make them sleepy, they could always count on counting sheep together to do the trick!

They were pleased with how they conducted themselves. "Less work for the boss when we eat, sing, dance, play and work at the same time in the same place. But dumb Denny," they baa-ed, turning up the noses at him, "he goes and gets lost all the time. We think the boss really gets upset spending time searching for him. We're certain he'd prefer to stay with us instead of looking for that nerd! Ha! Ha! Then he hauls back big, dumb Denny stretched across his shoulders. And why? Obviously he doesn't trust Denny while Denny thinks it's all so great. He's got that silly grin on his puss. As if the boss thought dumb Denny were special! Ha! Ha! Look how the boss humors him! Pretending he thinks it's great to have Denny back!"

"Ahh!" they signed. "We're grateful: we don't get lost; we don't smell. We're so right. No need to question anything. Now altogether, let's eat and drink and walk. Ready, 1,2,3, go!"

And poor dumb Denny? Tomorrow's another day to get lost, found, and carried back in celebration by the boss!

Sheep Story
Reflection

"Black sheep" is an expression describing a person who is different from the others in a family. In the scriptural passage the lost sheep could be the black sheep who strays from the others and needs the shepherd's guidance to step in line with the others. However, there is another way of viewing the black sheep straying from family or flock.

The black sheep doesn't have a herd-like mentality like the other sheep because this sheep doesn't conform to the norm of how a good sheep ought to behave. The black sheep is lost from the perspective of the sheep who do everything together because being conformists are what good sheep ought to be. But from another perspective the lost sheep is the adventurous, creative sheep who strikes out on his own and finds new paths which the other sheep never find.

The Greek word for sheep is *proboton*, or the forward walking animal. In a flock the sheep move in the same direction. But the black sheep breaks away from the flock and moves in a different direction. It's no wonder that the shepherd is willing to leave the ninety-nine sheep in search of the lost sheep. The black sheep shows leadership qualities which the other ninety-nine conformist sheep don't.

Denny is big, dumb Denny according to the other sheep, but Denny has seen a lot more of the world because he's so often "lost" his way. His experience has helped him to be compassionate towards others who have gotten lost.

The story tells us that getting lost is not necessarily a loss for those who appear lost. To stray from the others can mean one is creative or inventive. Being an anomaly in the group might mean not fitting in or being lost, but endearing to the shepherd who rejoices in finding what is lost, the creative, venturesome spirit.

⋙ CHAPTER NINE ⋘

OPEN INVITATION

Luke 14:12-14 He said also to the one who had invited him, "When you give a luncheon or a dinner, do not invite your friends or your brothers or your relatives or rich neighbors, in case they may invite you in return, and you would be repaid. But when you give a banquet, invite the poor, the crippled, the lame, and the blind. And you will be blessed, because they cannot repay you, for you will be repaid at the resurrection of the righteous."

One of the dinner guests, on hearing this, said to him, "Blessed is anyone who will eat bread in the kingdom of God!" Then Jesus said to him, "Someone gave a great dinner and invited many. At the time for the dinner he sent his slave to say to those who had been invited, `Come; for everything is ready now.' But they all alike began to make excuses.

    The elderly gentleman was a striking figure as he stepped lightly down the streets of their city. Dressed in a blue pin striped suit, a fresh red carnation in his lapel, a bowler hat tipped slightly to the left, white gloves, and highly polished shoes, his eyes twinkled and his smile was inviting. Still the people he met thought him to be something of an eccentric—according to their standards. And why was that?

    He loved to throw parties and invite as many people as possible; nothing unusual about that. Lots of people love to throw parties. What was unusual is he sought out complete strangers. Even more unusual, he chatted with them as if he had known them for years.

    On the lookout at busy intersections, he'd tap someone's shoulder, strike up a conversation about the weather, the traffic, or the latest news, and add, "It's my wife's birthday. C'mon over and celebrate. We'd love to see you. The party wouldn't be the same without you. If you decide to come, give me a call." Dumbfounded, the person whom he invited was speechless or fell into stuttering, "I, I, I, I" since he couldn't recall having ever met the gentleman. And as happens with people who know us without our recognizing them, the person would be too embarrassed to ask the gentleman his name. Before there was time to say anything, the man pressed his card into the person's hand, tipped his hat, and disappeared into the crowd.

Often the gentleman invited several persons at a crack. For example, after he'd gotten a hair cut at the barber shop, he'd stand and announce to the other customers, "Hey, I'm throwing a party for my friend who's ninety years old tomorrow. C'mon and celebrate. We'd love to see you. The party won't be the same without you." Then he'd pass out calling cards and say, "If you have any problem finding my place, give me a buzz, and I'll give you directions." Having tipped the barber generously, he'd wish them well, wave goodbye and leave the shop. The startled customers looked at one another, shrugged their shoulders, and wondered who this man was that invited everybody to a party for a ninety-year old man. Like their customers, the barbers were also in the dark, since they had never seen the gentleman before.

Over and over he'd invite anyone he met to parties he was throwing for persons that nobody else seemed to know. No one ever knew when he'd show up. He'd appear in offices, factories, and supermarkets. Or he'd wave them down at entrances and exits to shopping mall parking lots. Nor was it unusual to meet him at symphonies and band concerts. He startled actors, musicians, and ballerinas—slipping them invitations as they waited in the wings to perform. The invitations were to parties for elderly people confined to nursing homes, lonely immigrants newly arrived from countries nobody knew existed, homeless nobodies in food shelters, and even shady ladies working the night shift on neon lit street corners. While the reasons for the parties varied, the old man's line remained the same. "We'd miss you if you didn't show. The party wouldn't be the same without you. Everybody will be expecting you." Then routinely he'd give his calling card and be on his way.

Often he invited folks whose presence he had previously sought but who refused his invitation. As time went on, these people grew hostile because they felt he had interrupted their privacy. They'd think, "He can't mean me. Why me? What's he up to? He doesn't know me. There's something fishy going on, and I don't like it. The old goat must be crazy! Besides, I don't know what kind of characters I'd meet at his parties; either losers or eggheads who'll make me look like an idiot! Better to play it safe and stay home."

But every so often one of those who had refused an invitation would see a friend who had accepted one and had gone to the party. Out of curiosity the person asked his friend whether the old man was there and what the party was like. The friend said, "Oh, the old man was waiting at the door alright! His face glowed and he was delighted that I came. Even though the place was crowded, I honestly felt I was the person he had been waiting for. But when I told the other guests how I felt, they said they felt the same way I did when he opened the door."

Feeling he had missed out on a great party, the person then asked his friend what they had been celebrating. His friend thought for a moment and then with a puzzled look said, "It was for a little crippled girl who had just gotten some braces for her legs. But I had the strangest feeling that the party was as much for me as it was for her."

Still, many of the other folks who kept getting these invitations invented excuses for not going to his parties. They told themselves they had more important things to do than go to parties for people they didn't know, were unimportant, or downright immoral...like those shady ladies who worked the night shift! Why waste precious time at parties for silly reasons?

Some of them were determined to give the old man the cold shoulder if he ever approached them again. For example, one young woman was standing in line at a checkout lane in a grocery store. As she stood there glancing through the latest gossip in the National Enquirer, she happened to look up and see the old man waving at her from one of the other lanes. Hearing the familiar words, "Hey, I'm throwing a party..." she winced, pretended she hadn't seen him, and began flipping furiously through the Enquirer. This didn't stop the old man. "I'm throwing a party for a friend of mine who's in prison. He could use a little cheering up. We're going there to celebrate. We'd love to see you. The party wouldn't be the same without you! You'll feel right at home!"

Mortified, as twenty pairs of inquiring eyes from all the lanes stared at her, she muttered, "What nerve! Me feeling right at home in a prison with them!" Abandoning her food cart and fanning herself with the Enquirer, she marched out of the store.

That same afternoon another woman was shopping for clothes in a department store. As she admired a dress on a mannequin near the front of the store, she happened to notice someone outside of the display window trying to get her attention. Guess who it was? The gentleman, dressed fit to kill in his pin stripe suit, bowler hat and white gloves. He was waving arms and hands wildly at her. Horrified, she looked directly into the lifeless eyes of the mannequin and pretended to be carrying on a conversation. Unaware of the growing number of customers alarmed by her behavior, she desperately tried to avoid the old man's signals. "Thank God I can't hear him," she whispered. "Just another party...inviting me...telling me how much I'd be missed! Tsk! Tsk! Nonsense! He's crazy! I'll just keep talking to this dummy!"

But the gentleman was so intent on inviting her that some of his words sailed through the open door of the department store. "C'mon over...for a friend...for you,....for you....for you..." So absorbed had she become in her conversation with the mannequin that she did not see him desperately pointing to her as he cried, "Party for you...for you. We'd miss you!"

Sadly, the old man shook his head and walked away. The woman, on the other hand, was perfectly content to be by herself as the mannequin seemed to return the compliment by smiling dumbly into the woman's eyes which had now glazed over. With a hint of sadness in her voice, the woman touched the mannequin's hand and said, "Who needs parties anyway?"

Open Invitation
Reflection

The gentleman indiscriminately invites everybody he meets to his parties. But many who are invited are discriminating about whom they'd like to be with at his parties. So they turn down his invitations repeatedly. Those who accept the invitation are surprised that they feel the party is as much for them as it is for those for whom the host is throwing the party. And this is the paradox. The gentleman announces the person he wishes to honor in a special way, but at the same time all the guests are each treated as if he or she were that special person.

Jesus invites all the rejects, the losers to table fellowship and treats each one as the honored guest. Why?

In his baptismal experience Jesus felt singled out as someone special, God's beloved Son. Did this inspire this peasant's son to preach to the others, the least, that unbeknownst to them they too were special in God's eyes? As Jesus' brothers and sisters they also were God's sons and daughters.

And if this was Jesus' inspiration, isn't it

challenging us to do as Jesus did? We, too, are called to play the host by inviting the lost and losers of this world to the fellowship he initiated.

❧ CHAPTER TEN ❧

TALENTS

Matthew 25:14-30 The case of a man who was going on a journey is similar. He called in his servants and handed his funds over to them according to each man's abilities. To one he disbursed five thousand silver pieces, to a second two thousand, and to a third a thousand.

"Hi!" Louie smiled and waved at people in expensive cars, beat up jalopies, taxis, school buses, 18-wheelers and pickup trucks. It didn't matter whether the passersby were seniors, teenagers, school children or hefty truck drivers. Louie had been greeting people on his street corner every day for forty years. That is all he did!

When he first started, people called him

screwy Louie. "Why's he doing that? What's he smiling for? Who's he saying hi to?" they asked as they craned their necks for a better view. "You're mental! They ought to lock you up," were the cruelest comments a few ignorant people hurled at him as they sped by his corner. But gradually those who regularly drove past Louie began to anticipate his familiar greeting. Sometimes a husband and wife who had been arguing called a truce just long enough to wave and comment on Louie's greeting. Chubby cheeked boys and giggling girls waved wildly on their way to school in yellow buses. Occasionally a matronly looking woman stopped her car and handed Louie a box of chocolate chip cookies.

Yes, Louie had been saying hi for forty-four years. Brain damaged as a baby when he fell out of a crib, he had spent his childhood playing quietly with his toys. When he became a teenager he did nothing else but rock away his time and look at pictures in comic books. Louie's parents had long ago despaired of Louie doing anything constructive. "Let's face it" his dad harped whenever the subject came up. "Louie has no future. He'll be looking at comic books forever."

Louie's parents were grateful they had at least one son who showed real promise. Lenny, their youngest, had brains and good looks.

"I'm gonna be a lawyer. You wait and see," he promised his folks.

"Our son's going to be a lawyer. Just wait and see," they bragged to relatives, neighbors and anyone who cared to listen. There wasn't much they could say about Louie and they felt embarrassed describing his preoccupation with comic books. Nor were they interested in discussing their middle son, Larry. "We hope he grows up some day. All he does is sit around, talk for hours on the phone to his girl friends, and raid the refrigerator," they sighed. "Oh yeh," they added as an afterthought, "Larry likes to go into Louie's room, wave and say 'hi' to him." Then they'd laugh. "He thinks Louie is actually going to answer him some day. What a pair of losers!"

One day when Larry was bounding past Louie's room, he leaned in, smiling and waving and, as usual, cheerily bellowed "hi". Then, as he turned to split, he thought he heard a quiet "hi" come back to him. Wheeling back, Larry cried, "Louie, you said hi!" This time Louie smiled, waved and said more loudly than before, "Hi!" Larry was beside himself. He dashed over to Louie, hugged him, ran out of the room and told his folks.

They were pleased, but certainly not elated. "Isn't that nice," they agreed. "Our son can say 'hi' at last. Let's hope he can learn more—complete sentences." They were happy for him but of course a wave, a smile and a 'hi' didn't come close to what their son Lenny would accomplish one day when he became a lawyer. Larry, on the other hand, marveled over Louie's accomplishment and his role in getting Louie to respond. He decided then and there to make a career out of helping people with problems similar to Louie's.

"Well, of course, it's better than doing nothing,"

his folks conceded when Larry told them what he intended to do. And in the privacy of their bedroom they observed, "He'll never succeed like Lenny, but there isn't anything we can do about that."

Lenny had the brains and the looks all right. He also had the gift of gab. "I'm gonna be a lawyer. You just wait and see!" Everybody waited.

Louie, on the other hand, wasted little time using his new found talent. He took his next big step when he put his comic books on a shelf, walked to the front door, opened it, and stepped out onto the porch. There he waved at letter carriers, kids delivering papers, bill collectors, neighbors—making them all feel welcome. Pleased with his success, he finally strode proudly to the corner of his block where a new world eagerly waited his presence, his talent.

And among the many persons who waved every day to Louie, was Larry as he drove to the hospital where he worked as a physical therapist for children.

As for Lenny, if anyone cared to look closely enough, on any afternoon he could be seen muttering from a swing on his porch, "I'm gonna be a lawyer some day. You just wait and see!"

TALENTS
Reflection

This story illustrates that the least among us are capable of doing much if there are people in our lives who believe the most can be made out of the least. Larry consistently greeted Louie and Louie's unexpected response one day developed into a ringing affirmation of the world and the people in it.

However minimal we consider our own or others' talents to be, this does not excuse us from developing our own or empowering others to develop theirs. True, Jesus proclaimed to the least, the losers, and the lost in his society that it was they who would be first to enter the Kingdom. But what emerges in the story of the talents is that we are challenged to develop all of the gifts we are dealt. This entails risk. It involved risk when Louie left the safety of his room and opened the door to the outside world. It involves risk for us when we leave the safety of our daily lives and enter the greater world.

≫ CHAPTER ELEVEN ≪

DANGEROUS AFFECTIONS

Matthew 8:28-29 When he came to the other side, to the country of the Gadarenes, two demoniacs coming out of the tombs met him. They were so fierce that no one could pass that way. Suddenly they shouted, "What have you to do with us, Son of God? Have you come here to torment us before the time?"

    They held hands as they strolled through the village; nothing strange about that. Many of the other men in the village held hands as they chatted while their wives remained dutifully at home. This was perfectly acceptable behavior. It would be unusual if it didn't occur. It was simply taken for granted. Then what was it that disturbed the two respected elders, Izzy and Jake, as they scrutinized the behavior of the men strolling through the marketplace? What had aroused their suspicion?

Among the villagers holding hands were two young men whose behavior was different from the others. Izzy was the first to spy the men passing by. Nearly spilling his coffee as he and Jake sat at a table in front of a café, a stunned Izzy whispered, "Did you see what I saw? Those two men looked affectionately at one another?"

Shocked, Jake whispered back, "No!" .

"Oh I kid you not. I wouldn't make it up! If we sit here long enough, they might come this way again and you'll see for yourself," Izzy assured Jake. On guard that something unusual, maybe even dangerous was happening, the elders scanned the crowded bazaar for the young men who had passed by earlier. Within minutes Izzy, who had the uncanny ability of noticing anything strange in people's behavior, elbowed Jake that the suspects were a stone's throw away. "Look, look! There they are. Do you see? Do you see? Didn't I tell you?" he cried triumphantly!

"I do, I do," Jake nodded. "They're looking at one another....in a way we don't see other men doing. This is disturbing, very disturbing!" No doubt the elders judged these men were doing something entirely out of place. Both agreed holding hands was perfectly normal—entirely acceptable. It always had been. It always would be. But affectionate glances toward one another? That called for an investigation!

"They're crossing boundaries. And you know

where that can lead?" Izzy added ominously.

"Chaos!" Jake gasped.

"You betcha! Unchecked, this could spread like wildfire among the men in our village."

"And if it did it wouldn't be long before it could contaminate our neighbors to the north and south!"

"Ohhh!" Beating their breasts, they slumped in their chairs at the prospect of so many men looking affectionately at one another. For a moment they were speechless. Rapidly rapping their fingers on the table, they considered what they as watchdogs of tradition were obliged to do. They trembled, trembled as they contemplated the potential disaster at hand. They had to act soon!

Finally Izzy spoke up. "We'll corner them and tell them they're out of line! We'll give them a chance to explain themselves. Hand holding, yes. Looking affectionately at one another, no."

"Just what I've been thinking," Jake agreed. "Tell them they're out of place. Hand holding, yes. Looking affectionately at one another, no. If they should refuse....well, we'll know what to do just as we've known what to do with others who've strayed from the righteous path!"

"So be it! Let's find them now before any more damage is done! Plug the hole in the dike before it's too late" Izzy warned. Rising, he grabbed Jake's hand and they marched off to straighten out these deviants.

It wasn't long before they spotted the men. Determined to fulfill their god given duty and prevent impending chaos, they intercepted them as they were about to enter a small shop in the bazaar. "You can't do that! You cannot do that! It's an abomination!" Izzy blurted.

"What?" the men puzzled.

"It's an abomination! It'll lead to chaos! We'll be the laughing stock!" Izzy continued.

Confused, one of the young men asked, "What are you talking about?"

"Looking into one another's eyes...that wwway!" Izzy sputtered.

Still confused, the young man asked, "Which way?"

"Ahhh – fffectio—nately!" he stammered as if the very mention of the word were dangerous.

"So...what's wrong with that?" the man asked innocently.

"What's wrong? What's wrong? Well, well, well..." Izzy was momentarily at a loss to explain what these men were doing was so terrible. But Jake came to his defense.

"It's immoral! Unnatural! Dirty!"

"Dirty?"

"Yes, dirty! GOD NEVER INTENDED IT!" Jake knew he held the winning card. God never intended it. Surely that would convince these men how dirty they had become.

"Really? Looking affectionately at one another is something God never intended. That's news to me."

"It's unhealthy! Unwholesome! Keep it up, and..."

"And?"

"You'll see! You'll learn to regret what you're doing." Then grabbing Izzy's hand, they turned abruptly on their heels and walked away.

The two young men shrugged their shoulders as they wondered what was in store for them since they had no intention of taking the elders' advice.

It wasn't long before they began to discover the consequences of their behavior. As they walked the streets of the village, they noticed more and more of the villagers ignored them. Their greetings were met with stony silence, and they found it more and more difficult to purchase bare necessities. "Unclean - Not Wanted," signs immediately appeared as they approached places of business in the village. At first, they wondered what they had done to deserve this treatment. Feeling more and more isolated, they sadly recalled the elders threat if they continued looking affectionately at one another.

Gradually the feelings of affection they shared were overshadowed by feelings of guilt. Though they couldn't understand why they should feel guilty, these feelings weighed so heavily on them that they couldn't find any rest. As the days and weeks passed, they felt alienated not only from the villagers, but from one another. Looking haggard and distraught, they fled from the village and wandered to a place known as the Tombs—a place of death. Daily they wailed and berated themselves for the terrible feelings they had had for one another.

It was on one such day that a man visited the

tombs. He was clothed in a white tunic. Preoccupied with their guilt, the men didn't notice him. Seeing him, they cowered before him for they were fearful he, too, would tell them how wicked they were. But he did not. Instead he smiled and greeted them. "May I spend some time with you?" he asked. They didn't know what to say since no one had greeted them, or spoken to them for months. "May I spend time with you?" he asked again. Still they said nothing. This did not deter him as he came closer. The men froze.

"What do you want of us? Have you come to harm us?" they cried.

"Harm you? Oh no, no!" the man said softly. By this time he was kneeling beside them. "I'd just like some company. These past few days I've been lonely wandering through the country. Then I saw you from the road as I was passing by. That's why I'm here. Is that okay?" Without waiting for an answer, he extended his hands to them. For a moment they didn't know what to do since it had been so long since they had had any physical contact with anyone, including each other. But his smile was so inviting that slowly each extended a hand to him. Gently he received their hands in his, and as he did, they formed a circle. The longer he held each man's hand, the more the men felt at peace. Then he did something that surprised them both.

He invited them to hold each other's hand, and look into each other's eyes. "You'll be surprised what you see!" he said. They hesitated, because they already knew the pain they had suffered from doing what he invited them to do. But he spoke with such assurance that gradually they looked into one another's eyes. "What do you see?" he asked. Without waiting for an answer he said, "Someone worth loving? Someone good? I think so." The two men looked into one another's eyes. Tears rolled down their cheeks as if they were waking up from some terrible nightmare in which they felt guilt for seeing in one another someone they deeply loved, and now recognized as beautiful.

"Don't let anyone persuade you that your feelings for one another are wrong" the man said. Once more holding their hands, he looked at them affectionately. They wondered who this stranger was who hadn't judged them, but had shown them so much affection. For this they were grateful.

They were no longer alone.

Dangerous Affections
Reflection

What do we think of two men looking affectionately at one another? If we're coming from a tradition where men assume holding hands is acceptable but anything beyond that is unacceptable because not traditional, then mutual affection is unacceptable since it threatens the stability of tradition.

On the other hand, if we ask ourselves whether looking at one another affectionately deepens one's ability to love and care for one another, then we can entertain the possibility that a healthy tradition is able to integrate new insights on what it means to be human. If the tradition cannot do this, then the tradition itself becomes dehumanizing.

We might feel uneasy about this story if we think these men were up to more than mutual affection. That they had more in mind is a possibility. But the focus in the story is why the elders thought what these men were doing to be objectionable. It is their nonconformity. Because they didn't conform, they were alienated from the community. Then they were alienated from one another because they had internalized the community's negative attitude toward them, resulting in their experience of unbearable guilt.

What Jesus asked them to see in each other is what they had ceased to see, namely, goodness. Jesus' compassion was at odds with a community that ostracized them and left them no choice but to become citizens of the Tombs, the place where they were lost to the community, and tragically to one another.

Demonstrations of simple affection between men today might meet with strong disapproval and even death in many parts of this country where Christians sing, "They will know we are Christians by our love." Traditions still have the power of being destructive. Jesus knew this and questioned the value of a tradition if it inhibited people from being the people God had called them to be. A healthy critique of tradition is always necessary, especially if it prevents individuals or certain classes of individuals from giving and receiving love as other members of a society.

➢ CHAPTER TWELVE ➢

HEALING TOUCH

Mark 5:24-28 And a large crowd followed him and pressed in on him. Now there was a woman who had been suffering from hemorrhages for twelve years. She had endured much under many physicians, and had spent all that she had; and she was no better, but rather grew worse. She had heard about Jesus, and came up behind him in the crowd and touched his cloak, for she said, "If I but touch his clothes, I will be made well."

Cynthia had been bleeding from the uterus for twelve years. According to the purity laws, once the bleeding began, she became an untouchable. Since women were already considered less clean than men, and a continuing threat of polluting them, her bleeding further isolated her. What was more distressing is the bleeding began when she was engaged to be married. When she told her fiancé of her condition, he called off the engagement. Unfortunately, she had no brothers to look after her or protect her interests.

Ever since she was a child Cynthia had been fun loving and affectionate. But once the bleeding began, she could no longer touch or be touched by others. Even the doctors whose help she sought wouldn't touch her. Instead, she suffered the indignity of doctors probing her body with cold instruments as if she were a machine. Cynthia's hunger for intimacy deepened. But the force of law, and her observance of it, dampened any hope of intimacy. Like other women she was obliged to submit without question to the law's claims.

As the years passed, her hope for a cure diminished while her medical bills mounted. Not only did the bleeding continue; it got worse. One day, however, a crisis ensued which would change her life. Increasingly, she felt torn between her desire for intimacy and observing the law. She began questioning whether God intended laws that restricted giving or receiving love. At first she felt guilty that she had questioned the laws she had faithfully observed. However, as she wrestled with this dilemma, she began noticing what she hadn't noticed earlier.

Her eyes fell on others like herself, other people who were considered unclean. During the evening hours, when there were fewer people on the streets, she would slip out of her home and stroll in places where respectable citizens wouldn't go. There she'd come across other untouchables: beggars huddled near abandoned buildings, women like herself shielding their faces from suspicious glances, as well as the blind and crippled gingerly making their way down darkened alleys. The religiously observant carefully avoided the unclean. And when they couldn't, by averting their eyes, they'd pretend these untouchables didn't exist.

What Cynthia saw both angered and saddened her. "Observing the law makes no sense if this is what it's come to," she thought. "How can God possibly desire the observance of laws which bring such great suffering to so many? God is the Holy One, but isn't God also the Compassionate One?" Yet she observed that among the religious, the unclean hardly attracted anyone's compassion. Now she was convinced that God never intended any law to be dehumanizing. Though her convictions were strong, she was uncertain what to do about them until one evening when she took one of her late night walks.

Turning a corner, she saw a young man hobbling across the street. He leaned heavily on a crutch since he was missing a leg. Suddenly he fell, and the crutch landed beyond his reach. No one was there to help him. Like Cynthia, he too was considered unclean because he was physically defective. Quickly walking over to the crutch, Cynthia picked it up, brought it to him, and offered to help him get up. He was speechless that a woman would initiate a conversation with a man, and an unclean one at that.

"C'mon! I'll help you. It's okay," she assured

him. "I need the exercise!" Laughing, she bent over and gently aided the man as he got up. "Can you make it home all right?"

"Yeh, sure! Thanks, thanks a lot!" Touched by her concern, he smiled and hobbled a few yards down the street. Then he turned around, thanked Cynthia again, and continued on his way. She stood there for a few minutes, her eyes following the man as he disappeared in the dark. Choking up, she said, "The first time in years that I've touched anyone, anyone at all. It will not be the last!"

In the following months she gave sandwiches to startled prostitutes, sat and listened to their stories, hugged them and promised to return. She visited the poor living in hovels on the edges of the village. There, too, she shared whatever food she could spare as she listened to their stories.

She made a special point of visiting those whom everyone avoided—those with the ashen white, scaly skin. Holding their hands, she embraced them and thanked them for spending time with her. Then Cynthia would ask if she could return because they had been so helpful in cheering her up. She meant it, and they meant it when they told her that they felt a world of difference in her presence. In many instances the people whose lives she touched hadn't experienced anyone's touched in years.

Though she hadn't realized it, her life had taken on new meaning. A change had slowly taken place. No longer was she a submissive woman! She openly reached out to outcasts like herself.

What continued to drain her energy, however, was the bleeding. Although she no longer thought of herself as unclean, she still desired to be healed. Soon the opportunity for this occurred. Cynthia heard of a man called Jesus of Nazareth. She had seen his healing powers and his compassion. She had watched him from a distance and always wanted to meet him. But he was usually surrounded by large crowds which she still avoided. However, through reaching out to others, Cynthia now found the courage to dare what she wouldn't have done a few years earlier. She put her daring to the test one day when she heard that Jesus was in the neighborhood. It was mid afternoon.

Determined to find him, she wasn't quite sure what she'd do once she saw him. Looking out into her neighborhood she saw a large crowd. She guessed that Jesus had to be in the center of that crowd. Going out and drawing near, she thought if she could at least touch his cloak she might be healed. Taking a deep breath she elbowed her way through the crowd until she was directly behind Jesus. Quickly she touched his cloak. No sooner had she touched it than she felt energy pulsating through her body. She knew she had been healed!

"Who touched me?" Jesus thundered.

For a minute there was confusion as those around Jesus asked, "How should we know? Everybody's been touching you."

But Cynthia knew whose touch he meant. She had done what no other woman would do, touch a man in public. Trembling, she cried, "Sir, I touched you." Jesus swung around, facing her. Bowing, she continued, "I know you're compassionate, and if I were you I'd also be compassionate."

Jesus smiled. "I know you are compassionate. I've visited the places where you've been. The people love you." Taking her hand, he smiled. "Your faith has made you well. Go in peace. Continue to heal others!"

Cynthia's eyes welled up. He told her to go, and continue to heal others. That she would do. And she would joyfully proclaim how she had been healed by Jesus of Nazareth.

Healing Touch
Reflection

Does religion encourage or prevent intimate relationships among those who, through no fault of their own, have been labeled "defective" or losers by the elite within a religious tradition? Cynthia's hemorrhaging meant she was defective, and therefore incapable of entering into any intimate, physical relationship. She could not express her love or be loved as she needed and desired.

The crisis which she experienced is a crisis many marginalized people experience today. The elderly, those with physically handicaps, minorities, people seen as non-conformists or protesters, immigrants, illegal aliens, migrants, gay and lesbian people, transients, homeless, the unemployed, and frequently women, are seen as lesser, inferior members of the community, even though collectively they constitute an overwhelming majority of their communities. Does the Holy One then demand of them what the narrow religious elite define as being necessary for entering loving relationships? Or does God understand that the vast majority defined by the religious elite as lacking the integrity necessary to enter an intimate relationship; that these also have as much right to love and be loved as those considered whole?

While Jesus valued God as the Holy One, he also realized the danger of emphasizing God's holiness to the exclusion of recognizing the importance of God's compassion. Hence his mission was to preach compassion, a virtue we often hear preached but just as often not practiced towards those who don't conform, are a little off beat, or live a different lifestyle.

Would Jesus be uneasy with pronouncements today which call for others to lead angelic lives, instead of meeting their needs like other human beings who are encouraged to find fulfillment in loving, committed relationships?

CHAPTER THIRTEEN

WELL, WELL, WELL

John 4:7-8 A Samaritan woman came to draw water, and Jesus said to her, "Give me a drink." (His disciples had gone to the city to buy food.) The Samaritan woman said to him, "How is it that you, a Jew, ask a drink of me, a woman of Samaria?" (Jews do not share things in common with Samaritans.)

It was noon, and there was no one around to harass her as she left her house and walked down the empty streets. "A has been! Nothing left," she thought as she walked slowly to the well. Then she laughed. "A has been? I've never been anything to begin with. What do I mean? A has been!" That summed up her "life" as far as she was concerned. "And those husbands," she sighed. How could she possibly have thought any of them seriously loved her. They were interested in anything but her. She certainly wasn't a beauty queen now, nor had she been when she married her first husband. Other women might have attracted men because of their beauty or charm, but not her. She was appealing to him because of her family's wealth. He knew her dowry would be substantial, so he passionately professed his love for her. But it was her money he had fallen in love with. As to his other love, he was a philanderer who used her money to satisfy his sexual conquests of other women. However, he wasn't very tactful because he bragged of his affairs to others when he had too much to drink. It was only a matter of time before she found out and that was the end of that marriage.

      Her second marriage couldn't have been because of her money. Her first husband had taken care of that. There was little left after he had spent so much of it on other women. No, the reason she remarried is the reason so many remarry. Both were recently divorced. Both were lonely and needy. They thought by marrying they'd fill the void in their lives. Later she knew they ought to have known better. She realized they must have known in their hearts that marrying one another to fill this void wouldn't work. But they went ahead, and married anyway. For a while the marriage seemed to work since they always felt the need to be in one another's presence. But gradually they discovered their need was mutually smothering, since they placed demands on each other that neither could meet. The pressures increased and so, too, did the need to distance themselves from one another—permanently. Whatever love had been present died when they realized what they were doing to one another.

And number three? Why a third marriage? She wasn't sure. She thought maybe she had learned from her mistakes. Or had she become less and less concerned about making them? "Who knows? It could work!" she thought. Marrying became easier, but remaining married was no longer a sure thing. After all, past track records have a way of influencing the future. Failed marriages undermined her trust that she could succeed with this husband. Past failures haunted her as she tried working through the problems in her third marriage. However, not only did she feel she was failing but she blamed herself for her husband's failures. "It's not his fault," she told a friend. "It's mine. I've done what I've always done....mess things up!" She felt terribly guilty and her husband couldn't help her. He could only help himself. He wanted out. That ended number three.

One would think she wouldn't marry again. Why ask for more suffering? Yet in spite of feeling guilty over failed marriages, she still longed to be fulfilled by marrying again. Driven by this thirst she sought out anyone who offered the slightest chance of satisfying it. Desperate, in the marriages which followed, she settled for men who used and abused her. By the time she married her fifth husband she felt like damaged goods. Bruised and bloated from booze, she cared little how others thought of her—except that she didn't want to be known as a slut. But the men who married her to satisfy their lust confirmed what she feared. And now that she had left her fifth husband she had good reason to think of herself as a slut. She had recently taken up living with a man who was not her husband.

As she reached the well she thought, "A slut! Has it come to this?" She winced at the thought of it. Preoccupied with her thoughts, she hadn't noticed the man standing next to her at the edge of the well.

"Could you give me a drink of water?" he asked.

Startled, she looked up at the stranger. "What did you say?"

"I said could you give me a drink of water?"

"Here we go again," she thought. "Coming on to me this way!" She wanted to tell him that she was already spoken for; another man already occupying her bed at home. He'd have to wait his turn. But she was also intrigued by this man. He seemed different. She could tell by his accent that he wasn't a Samaritan. He was a Jew. That was a twist. A Jew. An enemy. She thought he must have been desperate or sensed that she was desperate. It didn't matter. "You a Jew asking me a Samaritan for some water?" She laughed. "You do know where you're at, don't you? This is a Samaritan village and you're talking to a Samaritan woman."

"I know. I know. But when you're thirsty, you're thirsty. And if you're desperate you'll go through five husbands to satisfy your thirst."

"What? Are you talking about me?" she asked defensively.

"About being thirsty or about the five

husbands?" he asked innocently.

"About being thirsty of course!" she shot back. But she knew it was as much about the husbands as it was about the thirst. "What's your angle?" she demanded.

"My angle? I don't have an angle!"

Didn't he? She wasn't convinced he didn't. But she thought it best to give him what he wanted. "Ok, Ok, I'll draw some water for you if that's all you want." And the woman slowly began to lower her bucket into the water. But as she did he said quietly, "Well there is something else!"

"Ah!" she thought. "Here we go! Yes?" she asked warily as she stopped lowering the bucket.

"That water down there. It's like everything else we thirst for. It never satisfies once and for all, does it?" She said nothing. He had hit home. He continued, "Maybe there's water in another well that satisfies completely."

"Oh!" she shot back. "Another well? This is the only one I know about!"

"The water I'm talking about is inside you."

"Inside me?"

"Yes, inside you! Ready to bubble up and over parched land just like this!" he cried as he stretched his arms and hands towards the desert.

There are times when someone's word taps into painful feelings—feelings of shame and guilt dwelling deep within. The stranger, a Jew no less, offered her the word that tapped into that well deep within. Slowly tears formed in her eyes, then the tears flowed freely, and she sobbed uncontrollably. And the stranger simply sat on the edge of the well. The only words he spoke were, "It's ok! Let it flow! Let it flow!"

And so she did. Not only did her tears flow but so too did her words of failure, despair, self-loathing, guilt, and shame. He continued listening to her story as she spoke of how miserably she had failed in all her marriages. "Five, if I'm not mistaken," he whispered.

"Why yes," she answered. But now she freely admitted what a minute earlier she couldn't acknowledge. Was it because in opening the floodgates of her past he didn't judge her? He listened and didn't judge. And as he listened she felt at peace with herself for the first time in years.

So at peace did she feel that she wanted to tell others how she felt and how this stranger at the well had helped her. Helped her? But how could she explain? That a Jew offered water which would bubble up within? That she told him everything about herself and he didn't judge her? That he knew more about her than she had told him? That what mattered more than anything was that he was there to listen? In her mind it didn't seem to make much sense, but still she felt the need to testify what happened at the well. "Sir, I have to go now. But I'll be back. Don't leave! There are others, many others who'll want to hear about this water bubbling up!"

The stranger smiled. "I'll be here. I'll be here." And she left to tell the villagers about the water in the well – the water that made her well.

Well, Well, Well
Reflection

More and more people are divorcing and remarrying. Much has been written why so many divorce today. What is unfortunate is that in spite of diocesan programs supporting those going through a divorce, persons who remarry are told they cannot receive the Eucharist unless they have their marriage annulled. Otherwise, they aren't fully integrated into the Catholic community. They remain second class citizens. The refusal to admit them to a place at the table is not only their loss, but ours as well.

It is strange that Jesus' policy of inviting everybody to open table fellowship has been prohibited today by religious leaders who preach Jesus' good news. Considering the number of Catholics whose first marriages weren't annulled, and who have entered second marriages yet continue to attend church, it seems callous not to invite the remarried to receive the Eucharist unless the remarried remain celibate by refraining from expressing their love sexually. We all know while this arrangement might satisfy angels, it is unlikely to satisfy human beings.

Jesus' presence to the Samaritan woman was a source of consolation to her, and a reminder that Jesus also ought to be available as a source of consolation today to other remarried persons attending the Eucharistic liturgy but still denied a place at the table. Sadly, denying Jesus' presence might also mean the remarried are lost to the community because they have been treated as losers, and have found compassion elsewhere.

≫ CHAPTER FOURTEEN ≪

SHAME

John 8:3-5 The scribes and the Pharisees brought a woman who had been caught in adultery; and making her stand before all of them, they said to him, "Teacher, this woman was caught in the very act of committing adultery. Now in the law Moses commanded us to stone such women. Now what do you say?"

"Shame on us if we don't uphold the law. We've the god-given duty to preserve it!" Abe reminded the other four watchdogs.

"Shame and more shame if we let anyone get away with breaking the law. No exceptions! Absolutely none," Izzy added.

"And that's why one of us has to follow up on the tip we've gotten about this adulterous affair in the making. One of us has got to see for himself exactly what's happening. So fellas I'll volunteer. It's no fun, but I'll make the sacrifice," Abe said, folding his hands and raising his eyes to heaven.

"Oh no!" Izzy protested. I'll volunteer. Why soil your eyes with the sordid details? I'm willing to bear the burden of having this foul deed burned in my memory."

"No, I'll do it!

"No, let me sacrifice! I'll do it!"

"No, I insist on doing it! I want to spare all of you the agony of watching this!" The other three were as insistent as Abe and Izzy that they would suffer watching the two get caught in the act of adultery.

"C'mon fellas," Abe pleaded. "We're getting nowhere with all of us offering to see what none of us wants to see. So let's all agree that all of us go to see the show, er, what's gonna take place." Abe's compromise was a brilliant display of logic which met everyone's approval to no one's satisfaction. Each would have preferred being the sole observer, but since that wasn't going to happen, the only option was for all to be there.

And where were they going? They had received a tip from a young girl's rejected suitor that she was bedding down with a man whose wife had left him. So when it was dark the pack silently huddled outside the man's bedroom window. They elbowed and stepped over one another as each struggled to get the best view—in the interest of the law of course!

When they were satisfied they had seen

enough - and enough never seemed enough - they broke down the front door and piled into the bedroom. Grabbing the girl they cried triumphantly, "Gotcha!"

"You're coming with us you slut," Abe said as the others pawed her body, and reluctantly threw a robe at her. The girl, about fourteen, blushed with shame. Even after she had covered herself, she frantically shielded her body with arms and hands since the pack couldn't resist eyeing her up and down. Powerless to cloak herself from their eyes, she felt even more ashamed.

And the man in bed? He managed to escape. Besides they weren't interested in him. It was the woman they wanted, even if she was only fourteen. And if convicted she could be stoned. As far as Abe and the boys were concerned she deserved it.

"It's off to court with you," Izzy said as he grabbed her arm while Abe grabbed the other. But they hadn't dragged her more than a couple of blocks when Izzy spied a familiar enemy in the distance. "Wait!" he said as he raised a hand for the pack to stop.

"What is it?" Abe asked.

"I have an idea," Izzy said. "I know how we can use our little slut to snare someone we've wanted for months!"

"You mean Jesus?" Abe asked excitedly.

"Yes," Izzy said. "Let's see what he thinks about our little bird. He's so soft-hearted we can get him to reject the law and make a fool of himself."

"Clever! Great idea! Brilliant!" they all agreed. So they hauled the girl before Jesus.

Jesus had been talking with his friend Philip. When he saw these men marching toward him, he was shocked at how they were treating her. From his past run-ins with them he knew they weren't up to any good. They paraded around as defenders of the law, but they were power hungry. And by the way they leered at her, they had something else on their minds.

"Ah, Rabbi, nice to see you!" Abe said as he greeted Jesus. But Jesus wasn't sidetracked by his greeting. He knew that Abe's only interest was tricking him into rejecting the law. The whole pack now encircled Jesus and the girl. She said nothing. Head bowed, she stood there frightened and ashamed.

"Rabbi," Abe began, "we have caught this woman committing adultery. In the..."

"You caught her in the act of adultery," Jesus interrupted. "All of you? At the same time? My, what a coincidence! Do you do this often?"

"Well..." Abe was momentarily caught off guard. Since he didn't know how to answer Jesus' questions he continued. "In the law Moses ordered such women to be stoned. What do you have to say about this case?"

Jesus paid little attention to their question. He knew what they were up to. Rather he looked at the girl, and guessed the shame she must have felt. He wanted to comfort her but he knew his words would simply draw attention to her, and deepen her shame. He didn't want this. He looked at Philip and smiled briefly. Philip had seen that smile before. He knew Jesus was up to something.

Jesus strolled about ten feet away from the

girl. As if he were going to map out some strategy to answer Abe's question, he knelt down and began drawing a large circle on the sandy ground. The pack strained to see what he was drawing. They knew he was up to something, but what? He drew another circle inside the big circle. And then another circle inside that circle. Then he began humming softly.

"What's he up to?" someone whispered.

"What's with all the circles?" another muttered to Abe.

"And what's with the humming? I've never heard him hum before," Izzy whispered in Abe's ear.

But Jesus wasn't finished. He erased the little circle and redrew it with his finger. The pack was growing more and more impatient. They were in the dark about all the circles he had drawn and they couldn't figure out what the humming had to do with the circles. What they didn't realize was that he had nothing more in mind than deflecting their attention from the girl to himself to relieve her of some of her shame. Even if he couldn't diminish it, he was determined not to intensify it.

Finally Abe had had enough. "Quit playing in the sand! Answer my question! Give us your opinion!" But Jesus ignored Abe. After he had slowly, very slowly drawn two smaller circles within the small one, he rose and stared at them, scrutinizing each one from top to bottom so that they felt naked in his presence.

Then he spoke. "Let the man among you who has no sin be the first to cast a stone at her." An interminable silence seemed to follow as he continued staring them down. While he did this some of the men lowered their heads, and shuffled their feet in the sand. Others looked off into the distance. All avoided his eyes.

The uneasy silence continued as Jesus again bent down and slowly began to erase the circles he had drawn. He never looked up. However, one by one Abe and the pack slunk away. They had come to shame him as they had the girl. And now ashamed themselves, they left. Philip walked a short distance away so that Jesus could be alone with the girl. She continued standing with bowed head.

Finally Jesus stood, gently raised her head, and said to her, "Woman where did they all disappear to? Has no one condemned you?"

The young girl's eyes flooded with tears. "No one, sir," she sobbed.

Jesus smiled and said, "Nor do I condemn you. You may go. But from now on, avoid this sin."

No longer did the young girl feel naked or ashamed. And she walked away—her dignity restored.

Shame
Reflection

There is nothing so alienating as feeling chronically shamed. The simplest way to define shame is by contrasting it with guilt. If we do something wrong we feel guilty about what we have done; but if we always feel deep shame about ourselves we see ourselves as defective. We don't simply do something wrong. We are wrong in our being.

In Jesus' day one could *be shamed*, and this refers to the publicly known loss of honor. This is negative shame. But to *have shame*, meant that individuals had a concern about their own honor. Biblical scholars, Malina and Rohrbaugh, write of the special importance attached to the sexual honor of a woman. While male honor was flexible and could sometimes be regained, female honor was absolute and once lost was lost forever. (1)

We can understand, then, why this story of the young girl is so tragic. Being shamed she became a lost cause, a loser.

The elders' attempt to shame Jesus is foiled as he turns the table and shames them because of their dishonorable attempt to shame both the girl and himself. His sensitivity to the girl's shame leads to her integration within the community.

People individually and collectively continue to be shamed today. Children can be shamed by parents who treat them as things rather than as human beings. Or they can be shamed because of their ethnic and/or race which is considered inferior by the racial or ethnic majority of a country. "Black is beautiful" is an expression which African Americans have used to counter negative attitudes directed towards them and often internalized by them as a result of racism within this country.

If someone feels chronically shamed so that he or she feels defective, then this person has become a loser in his or her own eyes. Jesus challenges us now, as he did 2,000 years ago, to affirm people rather than demeaning them as losers through shaming them.

(1) Bruce J. Malina and Richard L. Rohrbaugh, <u>Social-Science Commentary On The Synoptic Gospels</u>, Minneapolis: Fortress Press, 1992, p.77

❧ CHAPTER FIFTEEN ❦

TREE STUMP

Luke 19:1-4 He entered Jericho and was passing through it. A man was there named Zacchaeus; he was a chief tax collector and was rich. He was trying to see who Jesus was, but on account of the crowd he could not, because he was short in stature. So he ran ahead and climbed a sycamore tree to see him, because he was going to pass that way.

"Hey tree stump! What are we gonna do with you?" Cruel words, especially since they were from Zach's father. Verbally he assaulted Zach daily once he realized that Zach wasn't going to grow any bigger than 4' 8". It didn't matter it wasn't Zach's fault he was unusually short. What mattered was he had stopped growing, and his father blamed Zach. His father was embarrassed to walk anywhere with him because he felt Zach's height dishonored him. "I know what they're saying behind my back," he told Zach's mother. "What did I do to deserve a son no bigger than a tree stump?" Unfortunately, all of Zach's brothers and sisters were taller than he by at least a foot. While they didn't belittle Zach, they were fearful of contradicting their father. So they said nothing when Zach's father was upset.

Nor did Zach get any sympathy from the kids in the neighborhood. "Hey stump! When did ya stop growing? When you were two?" This hurt Zach more than anything. The kids his age were all bigger than he was, and they taunted him whenever he walked down the street.

"Stumpy boy, your rump is draggin' on the ground. Don't wear it out! Ha! Ha!" No one his age befriended him, and the grownups whispered how odd Zach looked whenever they saw him.

"Zach's done something horrible. That's why he looks like a tree stump!" they gossiped. He was painfully aware of their comments as he hurried past their houses.

He grew angrier each day because he was too short to fight the bullies who pushed him around. Nor was he able to tell the adults what he thought of their stinging remarks. He knew he'd be in for more trouble if he mouthed off to them. Besides being angry, he was ashamed of himself since he didn't think he was any better than a tree stump! But his anger stoked his desire for revenge against all who treated him poorly. However, it wasn't until he was in his early twenties that he had the opportunity for revenge.

He heard that the Romans occupying his country sought someone who could fill their coffers with money collected in taxes from the Jews. Since the Romans were so hated, they decided it was better to get another Jew to do their dirty work. Better a hated Jew than a hated Roman! "Hmmm, taxing the folks who've made my life hell! Sounds perfect," Zach thought. "They've treated me like dirt. Now it's my turn to throw some their way." Wasting no time, he marched to the Romans' command post to offer his services.

At first the Romans were skeptical that someone so short could collect taxes from the villagers. But as he spoke bitterly about the villagers, the Romans knew they had their man. They were delighted! He wanted revenge so badly he'd do anything, even if it meant squeezing the last coin from every village widow.

Zach's career as a tax collector had begun. At every house he visited he'd gleefully tell the startled occupant, "Remember me? The stump himself! Now let's see what taxes you're gonna cough up for ole' stump to give our Roman buddies." He savored the moments when he extorted money from angry villagers. It was payback time for him. And the villagers couldn't retaliate, because if they did he'd tell them, "Gee, I think you owe a little more than I thought."

Zach rubbed his hands together. Not only was he getting revenge, but the Romans were so satisfied with his work that they made him the chief tax collector in the village. They placed him in charge of a cadre of young tax collectors so they could learn the tricks of the trade. Zach had become a rich man, and he strutted around as if he were Caesar himself. No wonder the Romans referred to him as Little Caesar! They fed his ego by reminding him daily what a big man he had become. These constant reminders served to motivate him to continue being the best tax collector in the village. But "Little Caesar" was about to have an experience which would turn his life upside down.

On one of his visits he met a family whose parents had several sons and daughters. Among them was a young man named Jeremiah. What surprised Zach was that Jeremiah was an inch or two shorter than Zach. "And I thought I was the only stump in the village," Zach muttered. But what surprised him even more was how this family treated their son. They neither made fun of him nor treated him differently from themselves. No one singled him out for special treatment. "Nobody by the name of tree stump here!" Zach sighed.

He was so impressed with the family that he didn't check every nook or cranny to assess what needed to be taxed. And he felt comfortable with them because they didn't gawk at him as if he were an oddity. Of course, like the other villagers they weren't fond of tax collectors, but at least they didn't make Zach feel uncomfortable. He told them he'd return in a day or two to inform them how much tax they owed. But it was also an opportunity to get to know them better.

When he returned he drew the father aside, and asked him about Jeremiah. His father understood why Zach would ask about Jeremiah as he looked at this man, only a few inches taller than his son. Quietly he told Zach that Jeremiah was one of the most compassionate persons he knew, and he figured it might be because of his height.

"His height? Why his height?" Zach asked.

"My son has had to put up with bullies and gossips who have labeled him as weird or abnormal. But this has made him more sensitive to others who have been treated unfairly. My son is very tall in my eyes because of what he's endured, and he's a better person for it."

Zach choked up at this man's pride in his son, and his own father's feelings towards himself. He was so moved he didn't have the heart to ask Jeremiah's father to pay any taxes. Instead, he thanked him for his family's hospitality and left. But he had a lot to think about—especially how the villagers' ridicule had led him to seek revenge and led Jeremiah to be compassionate.

He walked in the park and sat on a park bench for hours thinking about these things. He covered his face with his hands and wept, because of what he had seen in this family and missed in his own. He was so absorbed in thought that he nearly missed seeing some villagers gather a short distance from where he was sitting. Curious on overhearing a villager mention that Jesus of Nazareth was preaching there, he thought, "Jesus, hmmm, I've heard of him. He's the fellow that's been dining with everyone under the sun including some of my own tax collectors! I wonder what he's up to? I think I'll go over and see if I can find out."

Zach walked over but the crowd was so dense it was impossible to see Jesus. "I should have known better! What's the use?" Zach said as he stood on his toes and saw nothing but everyone's legs. But then he noticed a sycamore tree about ten feet away. He thought for a minute, laughed, and said, "Well, well, so now I get to climb a tree! From being a tree stump to a tree climber! Is this progress or not?" He strolled over to the tree, climbed it, and scrambled out on a limb where he could see and hear Jesus. He almost fell off the limb when he caught sight of Jesus. He couldn't believe what he saw. Jesus couldn't have been more than a couple of inches taller than himself.

"Folks," he heard Jesus say, "it's who we are in God's eyes that makes all the difference in the world. No matter if we're tall or short, fat or skinny, God doesn't give a hoot! And why should he? The only small people in the world are the people who measure everyone else by their own standards and whine if they don't conform!" Then Jesus happened to look up and spotted Zach. Jesus laughed as he saw Zach wrapped around the limb. He shouted to Zach, "Isn't that right?" Zach didn't know what to say. He was overjoyed to hear so much wisdom coming from someone as short as himself. "I said," Jesus repeated, "isn't that right?"

"Right! Right on!" Zach yelled back.

Jesus laughed again. "You're out on a limb! Jump down. I want to come to your place for dinner. We've got a lot to talk about!"

At first he thought he hadn't heard Jesus right. Jesus wanted to come and join him for dinner? "My house?" he cried. "You want to come to my house?"

"You're the only one up in the tree I could be talking to!" Jesus said. That's all Zach needed to hear. He jumped off the limb and landed safely in Jesus' presence.

The crowd grumbled, of course. They didn't like the idea at all that Jesus was going to have dinner with this extortionist. But Zach wasn't thinking about the crowd's reaction. He had made up his mind that he was going to give up half of his belongings to the poor as a way of making up for the way he had treated people. He also decided to pay those he had cheated four times as much as he had cheated them. The events of the past couple days had affected him deeply.

Jesus looked at Zach and said, "Well we're both pretty short. Good! Now we can really see eye to eye on what needs to be done. Zach, salvation has come to your house today. Let's go!" Zach didn't know what Jesus meant exactly when he spoke of salvation coming to his house. But if salvation were anything like he had already experienced the past couple of days, then he was all for it. Zach wasn't a stump anymore!

Tree Stump
Reflection

Since Zacchaeus was a wealthy chief tax collector he would have been considered socially undesirable. Because he was the chief tax collector the people would also have thought him to be dishonest, and he would have had no credibility. In their eyes he was a lost soul.

Malina and Rohrbaugh point out that the gospel story of Zacchaeus is clearly a healing story because "salvation" which Jesus brings to Zacchaeus is his being restored to the community through Jesus' power. [1]

But in Tree Stump Zach is predisposed to Jesus' activity through discovering Jeremiah and how his adversity led him to be compassionate rather than bitter as Zack's adversity had made him. Zach also began to experience some communal acceptance within Jeremiah's family. We can see a process of transformation beginning in this family, and ending in Jesus telling Zach that salvation had come to him. This is the process of discovering that in others' eyes one is not lost nor a loser, but is respected and loved.

Many of us might experience similar transformations in our lives as we gradually feel less isolated and more welcomed by the different communities to which we belong. Salvation, or being integrated into our churches, or work places, or play spaces is dependent on persons who don't regard us as oddities or losers to be shunned, but as brothers and sisters who belong. The challenge of any community is to see beyond appearances to the person who feels lost and to welcome that person.

(1) Social-Science Commentary On The Synoptic Gospels, p. 387

⇶ CHAPTER SIXTEEN ⇷

SAVING NEED

Luke 8:1-3 Soon afterwards he went on through cities and villages, proclaiming and bringing the good news of the kingdom of God. The twelve were with him, as well as some women who had been cured of evil spirits and infirmities: Mary, called Magdalene, from whom seven demons had gone out, and Joanna, the wife of Herod's steward Chuza, and Susanna, and many others, who provided for them out of their resources.

John 20:15-18 Jesus said to her, "Woman, why are you weeping? Whom are you looking for?" Supposing him to be the gardener, she said to him, "Sir, if you have carried him away, tell me where you have laid him, and I will take him away.' Jesus said to her, "Mary!" She turned and said to him in Hebrew, "Rabbouni!" (which means Teacher). Jesus said to her, "Do not hold on to me, because I have not yet ascended to the Father. But go to my brothers and say to them, `I am ascending to my Father and your Father, to my God and your God.'" Mary Magdalene went and announced to the disciples, "I have seen the Lord'; and she told them that he said these things to her.

As a young wife and mother Mary loved to meet the needs of others. Whether it was looking after her bed-ridden mother, spending sleepless nights with crying babies, or responding to her husband's needs, Mary was always there. Being there for others was all she cared about. That she might have a deeper unfulfilled need never entered her mind. But years later, as she grew older and her family was less dependent, it was a different matter.

Now, practically no one needed Mary. Her mother had died. Her children were adults whose needs no longer included her daily services. And her husband seemed to need her only on special occasions. He was a busy man, a wealthy landowner who managed a large vineyard. And, when he wasn't managing the vineyard, he insisted on throwing parties in their mansion near the shores of the Sea of Galilee. He always assumed she'd be present at his side and look her best during these parties. Sadly, now his attitude made her feel like she was nothing more than another ornament in their home. In the past, meeting his needs as she had done might have satisfied her. It didn't anymore. Rather, it intensified a longing she herself couldn't comprehend.

Still, during his parties she would stand by, greeting guests, engaging them in light conversation, dining with them, and finally seeing them to the door at evening's end. And then... alone... Oh, her husband was there. But the party was over and so was his need for her. Besides, he was usually so tired he fell asleep seconds after they retired.

As for her friends? She had her social circle, but they were wives of her husband's business partners. Sometimes they politely invited her to their homes for social visits. But their words, "We'd love to have you" or, "We'll miss you if you don't show up," she never took seriously. She always thanked them for the compliments but she knew etiquette, not intimacy, dictated their interest in her. Slowly isolated, her feeling of not being needed or of only being needed for reasons which no longer satisfied her, took its toll.

She began to find it difficult to get out of bed in the morning. Opening her eyes at the early dawn, she'd stare at the ceiling until around noon when her husband demanded that she get some exercise. "It's for your own good," he'd say. But never did he spend time with her or say, "I love you." Even a semblance of love might have gotten her through the day. But since she couldn't recall him ever being affectionate she thought, "Why should he now?" Besides, "now" was too late!

Now she was possessed by an unknown dark power, which drained her of the energy to do anything. Often she sighed under its oppressive weight. Unconcerned about her appearance, she began to ignore her maid's plea to look presentable. What concerned her husband was how useless she had become to him; so he called in physicians from all over Galilee. After many examinations, they were all powerless to help her.

"She has everything she needs," they told her husband. "We recommend that she get the fresh sea air. Take her to the shore. Maybe the sea will help her."

"Of course," he said. "I'll bring her there. Better yet, since I've been busy lately, I'll have one of her maids take her."

"How thoughtful!" said the doctors as they left.

So daily the maid wheeled her to the shore where she was left to languish for hours. The sea breezes were of little help. She was still possessed by this dark power. Now words were few and hollow. Her maid dreaded having to sit with her for more than an hour at a time since Mary's dark mood was contagious. It affected the maid and all other visitors that might stop. However, since no one wanted to be with someone whom her husband described as useless, those who visited her were few. But there was one visitor who was different from the others.

It was during the maid's half-hour break one afternoon that a stranger walked along the shoreline. He approached Mary as she stared at the rolling waves. "Can you tell me where I can get a drink of water," he asked.

Mary didn't answer.

"I say...can you tell me where I can find some water to drink?"

Slowly Mary turned her head. Her eyes met his.

He studied her face and then said softly, "You look sad."

Mary's hand fell listlessly from her lap. The stranger knelt alongside the chair, lifted her hand, and instead of returning it to her lap, held it in his own.

"My name is Jesus," he said. "And yours?"

His touch sent a current of energy through her. "Mary," she whispered.

"Ahh, that's my mother's name," Jesus smiled. With his free hand he gently caressed her face. This startled Mary but she neither turned her face away nor raised a hand to stop him. He stroked her face so gently that each time he did, she felt more and more alive. Glancing over her shoulder at her home and the beautiful gardens surrounding it, he said, "You have everything you need....don't you? Everything, but my need for you."

"Your need for me?" she said. Her eyes searched his.

"Yes, life would mean much more if you were

with us...with me. I need you."

Mary's eyes glistened. She continued to feel his energy coursing through her body as he held her hand. "You need me? You really need me?"

"Yes."

Mary leaned forward. "Tell me more..."

And he did. He told her about his dreams for the future, how he was gathering others who shared his dreams, and his passion, and how others would help him make these dreams a reality. As he spoke she began feeling liberated from the dark power engulfing her. Was it his touch, or his vision, or both that was healing her? Slowly she rose from her chair, smiled, and whispered, "Please let me join you."

This was the beginning of her association with Jesus of Nazareth.

He needed her presence as one of his companions, and she needed him, especially whenever she felt herself slipping into the darkness from which she had been liberated. He'd take her hand, and hold it until she felt safe again. But when she felt he needed reassurance, she took his hand and held it firmly.

And the day he died? She was there along with a few others who needed him. More than ever, she regretted she couldn't caress his face, or touch his hand to bring forth life as he had done for her. But she was there for him. She would not leave him. "How strange," she thought. Though he was dying, it was life for her to be there.

No wonder, then, when he was buried she was the first to look for his tomb. She needed to be where his body was. No one could deprive her of being where they had laid him. But he wasn't in the tomb. And Mary wouldn't leave the spot. She was looking for him, and he wasn't there. Weeping, she sat on a rock.

"Why are you weeping? Who are you looking for?"

Startled, Mary looked up, and saw a man she thought to be the gardener. "Sir, if you're the one who carried him off, tell me where you have laid him and I will take him away."

"Mary!" he said.

"Jesus!" Immediately she recognized the voice. He was back! Or was he? Was her need for him so intense she imagined it was Jesus? It didn't matter. Overcome with joy she slipped off the rock to her knees and grasped his knees. Jesus smiled, bent over, and lifting her face gently with both hands said, "Mary, no need to hold on to me. I'm still here." Then lifting her to her feet he assured her, "I haven't gone yet. But I'd like you to go to our brothers and sisters and tell them I'll be going to our Father, your God and mine."

As much as Mary needed to be with Jesus, she realized how deeply he needed her to announce to whomever she could that Jesus had not abandoned them. His need, she thought, would now be her saving need.

Saving Need
Reflection

We are told that Mary Magdalene was possessed by seven demons. We don't know the nature of those demons. In Saving Need the demon is depression and Jesus heals her. Mary's importance in Jesus' ministry has been obscured because she is so often identified as a repentant prostitute whose life changed when she met Jesus. But there is no evidence in the gospel to support the notion that she was a prostitute.

Whatever the nature of her possession, she would have been considered one of many lost souls because she was possessed. In this story Mary's loss of what has defined her and the need to find her worth in meeting others' needs, leads to depression. Jesus' healing touch enables her to recover her worth as a person. There are different ways in which people lose and find themselves in another way. Certainly it isn't uncommon for someone whose self-worth is based on fulfilling others needs to go through the kind of change Mary experienced. Just as Mary found herself through Jesus' recognition of her worth as a person, it is important that others like Mary are acknowledged and celebrated as persons by others like Jesus.

In Luke's gospel she is mentioned along with Joanna and Susanna as one of the women who followed and financially supported Jesus in his work. Given the circumstances in Jesus' day that women were not to associate in public with men, Mary's decision to follow Jesus is remarkable. It is both a testimony to Jesus' openness toward women, and Mary's courage that she accepted his offer to become a disciple and follow him.

In John's gospel we read that Mary is the first person to whom Jesus reveals himself as the risen Lord. And he tells her to announce to the disciples that she has seen the Lord. We might say she gives the first sermon on Jesus' resurrection when she goes to the disciples and tells them what she has seen.

If Jesus were walking the earth today it is possible that he and Mary would need the same courage to have women take their rightful place in the church. If he asked her to preach the first sermon 2,000 years ago, undoubtedly he would ask her to continue preaching in the church today, especially against any attitudes or behavior leading to the loss of self-worth.

⋙ CHAPTER SEVENTEEN ⋘

THE VILLAGE OF CLEAN LIVING

Mark 6:7-8 He called the twelve and began to send them out two by two, and gave them authority over the unclean spirits.

They were excited. Two by two Jesus' disciples were to enter the villages, and spread the good news. Jude was ecstatic. "We're bringing great news—healing words!"

Bart agreed. "Yeh, and doing wondrous deeds—expelling demons!"

With nothing more than a traveling stick in hand, they began their journey. However, they had hardly gotten on the outskirts of the village when Jude complained, "I'm really thirsty. Let's stop for some beer!"

"How can we, Jude? We don't have a cent with us. We got rid of the money we had when Jesus told us not to carry so much as a penny."

"No problem, Bart. Let's ask this stranger for fifty cents." He pointed to a man coming their way. "Hey buddy, could you spare fifty cents for some beer?"

Disgusted, the man waved his hand. "No, why don't you fellas work instead of bumming around?"

"But sir," Jude tried to explain. "We've got this good news and..."

"The best news would be if you cleaned up and got some work," the man interrupted, and made a quick departure.

"Bums indeed! What nerve!" Jude grumbled.

"Well we don't have much of a wardrobe, do we?" Bart said, pointing to tunics already covered with dust. "The boss told us to wear one tunic and one only. Guess what people will be saying about us when they see us? These tunics will be pretty dirty."

"Who cares about a little dirt, Bart? What we've got to offer is more important than clean clothes. You've got to be confident!"

However, Bart's misgivings about what the future held seemed justified when they reached the little Village of Clean Living. No one was at the village gate to greet them as they had anticipated. Instead of a welcome mat there was a mat with large black letters which read "Wipe Your Sandals Before Proceeding."

"Hmmm," Bart wondered. "What kind of people live here?" It didn't take long to find out.

"Hey fellas, I'd watch it if I were you." Startled by an ominous sounding voice, Jude and Bart spied a man sporting a spotless tunic, gloves and sandals. He was leaning against a tree some twenty feet beyond the gate's entrance.

"What was that?" Jude asked anxiously.

"I said I'd watch it if I were you. This is the Village of Clean Living. What do you think people are going to say when they see you strolling into town in those outfits?" he asked, bringing his hand to his nose.

"Well, I..." Jude tried to answer.

"'The Dirty Boys are here. Get a whiff of them. They're polluting the air!'"

"C'mon, we aren't all that bad..." Jude protested.

"You're not squeaky clean and that's bad, real bad! Don't you know what's important in life? What the priorities are? What..."

"We thought we did..." Bart interrupted. "We're bringing good news. We've come to help people drive away misery and disease, deal with depressions and addictions, and offer a word of hope."

"Hey man, are you listening to me?" pressed the stranger. "This is the Village of Clean Living. Here we keep the mule crap off the roads, scrub and wash our kids, houses, garages and shopping malls! We voted to do away with dirt under our nails, on the stairs, and in the gardens—spent money to Astroturf our parks, yards, and cemeteries! Those are our priorities. You want to give good news? Sell us bushels of deodorants and multi-colored, multi-scented soaps that brighten up the flesh! Shower us with mouth rinses and teeth whiteners that give us the clean living look! Import cleaning fluids from neighboring villages! Don't get worked up over addictions, depressions, degradations or demons of any other kind! How absurd to be concerned about life's point and purpose when clean living is our delight!"

Jude didn't know what to say. He hadn't expected this kind of reaction to their message. "I think he's loony," he whispered. "He must have escaped from the local funny farm." Bart didn't answer. He wasn't as certain as Jude that this fellow was an exception to what lay ahead. "Let's say goodbye and move on," Jude continued.

Bart agreed. "Ah, nice talking to you but we've got to go now."

"Ok, ok, don't say I didn't warn you," the man cautioned, shrugging his shoulders.

Jude and Bart hurried past him and Jude sighed, "Phewww! Glad that's over!" However, they hadn't walked more than ten minutes when they saw an incredible scene. Dressed impeccably, men, women and children tiptoed warily on white washed sidewalks to avoid stepping on any smudge or hint of dirt. Homeowners bearing aerosol cans routinely marched out of their houses spraying the air after strollers had passed by. Sssst! Ssssst! Sssst! sounds punctuated the silence. Almost to a house, two or three members of the household were zealously cleaning windows inside and out. Trash bags were everywhere in sight as old men vacuumed the lawns, and emptied infinitesimal amounts of dust into the bags. Occasionally neighbors glanced over their picket fences to check on one another's progress. But when they saw Jude and Bart they gasped as they pointed disapprovingly at them.

"No one seems friendly," Jude remarked. "They don't talk to one another at all. They must spend every minute of the day trying to be clean. The man at the gate was no exception." Attempting to make sense out of what he had seen, Jude paused for a minute. He glanced across the street and saw a bench. "I've got to sit down for a couple of minutes. Let's cross the street and sit on the bench next to that uniformed man."

They crossed the street and were about to sit down when the man raised his hand. "Wait!" he ordered. He pointed to a sign on the bench. It read: *By order of the village government the following are forbidden to sit here: loiterers, dirty old men, people who tell dirty jokes, have dirty hands and dirty underwear.* After they had read the sign the man asked them, "Shall I tell you which of these applies to you or would you like to guess?"

Bewildered, Jude and Bart shook their heads and walked away. "You see why they've rejected us," Bart said. "To them we're not clean. We've got dust all over us and we smell terrible. Who we are and what our message is doesn't matter. What they care about is their version of clean living. And what they find offensive has nothing to do with being isolated from one another."

"What can we do?" Jude wondered.

Bart knew the answer to that question. "Jesus told us what to do. I'm ready to follow his orders although I'd be surprised to find any dust to shake from my feet as a testimony against this place. One day I hope we'll be able to return. For the time being we have to leave this village, possessed as it is by a powerful demon we can do nothing about.

Jude and Bart turned and walked away. Shortly thereafter an elderly man holding an aerosol can hobbled out of his house and sprayed where Jude and Bart had been standing.

Yes, the Village of Clean Living was possessed by a very powerful demon indeed!

Village of Clean Living
Reflection

The Village of Clean Living has a clean, collective persona. The people living there dedicate themselves to putting on a good front. What counts are appearances, not what is behind those appearances. Other stories in this volume single out individuals and groups of persons who present a clean persona but in this story it is impossible to find anyone other than the disciples, who isn't <u>obsessed</u> with being clean. And this is a powerful demon possessing the village because this obsession cloaks the village's shadow or its addictions, depressions, etc. which the disciples had hoped to confront. People don't relate to one another because they are too busy competing with one another to see who is cleanest—in appearances only! Does this mirror any community we might encounter in our society?

We expect crimes to occur in our inner cities but we are shocked when we read of abuses occurring in our suburban communities where people live in lovely homes surrounded by trees, lawns, and flower gardens which could serve as advertisements in <u>House Beautiful</u>.

It would be unfair to suggest that families living in these communities aren't concerned about priorities in their lives. But the Village of Clean Living is a reminder that people who are affluent might spend more time on appearances than matters of substance because they have the money to do so. And as the story suggests, they might also be less likely to express the need for healing because they are more preoccupied with what the neighbors think than with the real issues they need to address in their families and communities. If the obsession with being clean is a powerful demon in the village, the greater demon is that the people are completely unaware of how lost they are. Our ability to acknowledge that we don't know where we are or where we are going might dispose us to seek the help we need.

⇛ CHAPTER EIGHTEEN ⇚

BROKEN PROMISE

Luke 24:13-14 On that same day two of Jesus' followers were going to a village named Emmaus, about seven miles from Jerusalem, and they were talking to each other about all the things that had happened.

Life is a broken promise now that Jesus is dead," Cleo complained to his friend Eli as they walked on the road to Emmaus. "Or what's there to live for? Now everything has fallen apart." Twenty-five years earlier, Cleo had had such high hopes. "My future's promising," (he had boasted)."It's looking great! I'm going to find me a good looking gal. We'll get married, settle down, and have bright kids who'll really go places. And I'll own a business that will make me a mint." A promising future? That's what he thought twenty- five years ago. But now at age forty-five, it was a different story.

Cleo had gotten married but not to the girl of his dreams. True, she had pale blue eyes, ruby lips and a winning smile, but she also had a nose bent just slightly to the left. She cooked a good meal; but she couldn't sew a button on a shirt if her life depended on it. She had a good ear for listening but she wasn't much for talking. Humming was her long suit but she sang with a twang.

As for their marriage, sometimes they'd chirp along but just as often they'd growl. Smiling one day, they snarled the next. All in all the marriage wasn't bad but Cleo had had such high hopes—and now life seemed a broken promise.

And his children? The kids who'd eagerly listen to mom and dad's words of wisdom? The bright kids who were really going places? One was smart in math but dumb in spelling; the other was smart in spelling but dumb in math. They weren't bad looking but they had their mother's nose which bent just slightly to the left. As for listening to their parents' words of advice, they listened alright. Then they'd scratch their heads, shrug their shoulders and do whatever they wanted. Both of them moved to the other side of town and worked in the local glue factory. It didn't take much to make them happy. But

Cleo had had such high hopes for them and now life seemed a broken promise.

And the promising career? Cleo owned and operated a bagel bakery; not the smallest business in town but not the biggest. His bagels weren't bad, but they weren't the best either. He made money but not the mint he said he'd make. All in all, his was a modestly successful business. But Cleo had had such high hopes and now life was passing by. It seemed a broken promise.

As if to prove that "There's no fool like an old fool," well into his forties Cleo got suckered in again. This time he pinned his high hopes on Jesus of Nazareth. "Surely he won't let me down," Cleo thought. "Jesus is the one. He's the wave of the future. He's our promise. A real winner! His power base is here and he's going to drive the bully boys away. He'll make this a land of promise again and we'll be on the move." But the promised one was nailed to the tree and left to die a broken man. Hardly a winner and no one's future. Just another broken promise. And for Cleo, the last straw.

"I just don't understand," Cleo complained as he and his friend Eli walked the dusty road to Emmaus. "What went wrong? He wasn't supposed to die? That wasn't in the cards. Where's the winner we were promised? I'll tell you...nowhere! Sure, a couple of women report he's alive but that's absurd, impossible!"

"May I join you?"

"Wha...?" Cleo and Eli turned to see a man walking a few feet behind. "May I join you? I don't like walking this road alone."

"Suit yourself," Cleo said. "We were just talking about Jesus of Nazareth."

"Oh? What about him?"

"You mean you haven't heard the news?"

"I've been away for three days."

"Well, he's not what we'd thought. Just another flash in the pan, another broken promise." And Cleo proceeded to tell the man all that had happened not only to Jesus, but all the disappointments in his own life as well.

"Hmmm," the man stroked his chin. "Your story sounds vaguely familiar. About three years ago I was convinced that all of us: my friends, the people I talked to, myself—that we all had a promising future. Changes in our lives were to take place over night. The day would dawn when people from all over would sit around one table and enjoy each other's company. We knew we'd have to overcome certain obstacles. But we'd win out! We'd triumph! Life seemed so promising!" The stranger paused.

"And?" Cleo waved a hand.

"Well...not everyone shared our enthusiasm. In fact, some people were downright hostile! Even the friends we counted on most betrayed us." His voice grew raspy. "And worst of all, the one whose support and love I relied on most seemed to have abandoned me when I needed him most!"

"Really?" Both Cleo and Eli's eyes widened.

"Yes, when I was just hanging there, hurting, I said, 'Where are you when I need you?' And, you know, he said nothing. Nothing!"

"No kidding! So what did you do?" Eli asked.

"At first I thought 'That's it! There goes the future! Promises, promises! Right out the window!' I felt wretched and in a lot of pain. But then I thought 'So there's a change of plans. So it's not working out according to my expectations! I can't do anything about that. Ill just hang in there, wait, and trust it will all work out. What else can I do?'"

"And what happened?"

"I think I died."

"I know the feeling well" Cleo sighed.

"You what?" Eli was all in a muddle.

"I think I died," the stranger repeated, looking off into the distance.

"But...you're here. How...?"

"I'm here but...all I know is that the one whom I thought had abandoned me, pulled me through. And now I'm alive in a new way. Even my friends aren't going to recognize me right away. It's a changed ball game, believe me! Just when you think 'It's over. Life is just a heap of broken promises...' Surprise! Back alive in a way no one expected!"

"Hmmm, I never thought of it that way," Cleo said. Turning to the man he asked, "Have we met before? Your voice...your smile..."

"Maybe I resemble someone you know."

"Could be. Could be," Cleo said, trying without success to recall who this engaging young man resembled. However, they had reached Emmaus and the stranger told them he had to continue on his way. But Cleo and Eli persuaded him to join them at the bagel factory for a light lunch.

When they arrived, Cleo spread a white tablecloth over a workbench and placed on it a small loaf of bread, a carafe of wine and three goblets. Once they sat down Cleo invited the stranger to do the honor of breaking the bread. Taking the bread into his hands, the man ran his fingers over the small loaf. "Nice texture! Did you bake it?"

"Yes," Cleo answered. "This morning."

"Ah, freshly risen," he whispered, "and it smells so good." No sooner had the stranger spoken the word "risen" than Cleo's heart began beating faster. He remembered the stranger's words about coming alive in a new way and it struck Cleo how closely this man's experience paralleled Jesus'—his hopes, his betrayal, his death. And now...? Both Cleo and Eli's eyes were riveted on their guest as he broke the bread and shared the cup. When they had finished the meal the man said, "We know each other better now, don't we? I hope you will remember me whenever you break bread together."

"Yes," Cleo said softly. "We will." The stranger rose.

It's time for me to go. I have much to do. I have many friends with whom I'll be breaking bread. Thank you for your hospitality. Please stay sitting. I'll let myself out." And the man left the house. "It's him," Cleo whispered.

"I know," Eli said. Cleo rose, went to the window, and watched the stranger as he disappeared over the horizon. "He's come back, Eli. He's come back!"

Broken Promise
Reflection

Broken Promise is, among other things, a story not only about Jesus' disciples feeling like losers, but Jesus' own experience of feeling like a loser, and lost in relation to the one on whom he counted most as he was dying. Disillusionment or the loss of illusions of how one's life should turn out leads one to experience being lost. Cleo's life is riddled with disillusionment in his relationships.

As with Cleo, for us "Hangin' in there" expresses how we are getting along: how we're handling a job; working through a relationship; doing in school. For some of us hangin' in is not particularly difficult. We're pretty confident that we'll do all right; we'll manage. However, for others hangin' in there means being helpless and lost. We're not really sure if we'll survive a difficult time: a midlife transition or the loss of a loved one. The pain of just hangin' in there can reveal just how broken we are in body, mind, and spirit.

The times of just hangin' in there are frequently dark and depressing because they reveal how lost we feel. Yet, as our story suggests, hangin' in can also mean trusting and waiting. We wait and wait. For what? For something new to develop. For a break through brokenness. For transformation. For new life.

For Jesus "hangin' in there" is a transformative experience which leads him through death to life. He felt lost and then discovered God had never abandoned him.

For us, as with Jesus, trusting and waiting doesn't mean that after a period of hangin' in there we've finally found our way. It means we have reached an impasse and cannot find any way to stop hanging in. All we can do is trust that there is one who is with us as we hang and that, as in Jesus' hanging and dying, this one hasn't abandoned us.

Hangin' in there, then, is both a sign of our helplessness and the medium through which we can experience transformation from death to life. We do not experience this transformation because it has to happen, but rather because we believe that the one who raised Jesus from the dead has promised it will happen.

As the medium of transformation, hangin' in there is paradoxically darkness and light; it is a blinding light. We do not see a way out of our predicament and because we are blind we wait in the dark to "see" in a new way. Is waiting itself the first necessary step we need, to discover we have never been lost at all—that God does have the whole world in his hands?

Jesus' identification throughout his ministry with the losers and the lost paradoxically enables all who are lost and losers to find themselves in Jesus' company. Once we recognize we are all lost in one way or another, we too might discover God has never abandoned us in the first place.

⇛ CHAPTER NINETEEN ⇚

FIRED UP WITH THE GOOD NEWS

Acts 2:1-4 When the day of Pentecost came it found them gathered in one place. And suddenly from heaven there came a sound like the rush of a violent wind, and it filled the entire house where they were sitting. Divided tongues, as of fire, appeared among them, and a tongue rested on each of them. All of them were filled with the Holy Spirit and began to speak in other languages, as the Spirit gave them ability.

Before he died, Jesus and his friends often gathered in a room above an old, abandoned house. They were inspired by his dreams about the future as he broke bread with them. Later, as they grieved his death in this room, they drew strength from his presence when he appeared one evening from nowhere. They were relieved because he was with them again, and they were prepared to preach Jesus' good news to all.

But their excitement was short-lived. He said he had to leave, but that he'd return. But how or when, he didn't say. As the days passed and he didn't return, they hid in the room because they feared the authorities who plotted Jesus' death might also be plotting theirs. However they didn't openly acknowledge or address these fears. Instead they busied themselves about other matters. But something was about to happen that would change their lives forever.

"My head's hot! I gotta get out of here," Phil panicked as he paced the length of the room.

"Cool it Phil!" Pete was alarmed as he observed Phil's strange behavior. "You've got a fever from some kind of bug. That's all!"

"Yeh! Yeh!" Phil muttered. "But from what?"

"Just put a wet towel on your head, simmer down, and wait it out, " Pete said as he struggled to think of something, anything to calm Phil.

"A wet towel? You think that'll help? I'm hot, so hot that the towel's likely to steam up the place!" he cried, slumping in one of the chairs around the huge table.

Pete felt relieved when Phil stopped pacing. He remembered how this table had once been a center of joy, not a refuge for a disturbed disciple. Actually, the whole room appeared to be a haven for refugees. The huge windows were bolted shut, the drapes drawn, the doors barred and padlocked. Some heavy chairs had been propped up against the doors to insure the disciples' safety.

Phil's behavior hadn't gone unnoticed. The others were shaken up and nervously reminded Phil why they were there.

"C'mon Phil," Jim demanded. "Get serious! Settle down! We've got heavy duty stuff to discuss. We need to consider our options, and plan strategies..."

"And appoint committees to review those options," John added.

"Not to mention pondering the consequences of bad choices," Jim declared, "which of course would bring us back to the drawing board."

"You see," Pete added, "you can never be too careful. We don't want to throw caution to the wind, do we?" Then slowly, "We've got to take this one step at a time—*one* step at a time in an orderly fashion..."

Barely had he spoken the words "orderly fashion" than a cool breeze swept across the room overturning paper cups, plates, plastic knives and forks neatly arranged on the table. "Whew!" John shuddered, scanning the room. "Where's that breeze coming from? No cracks in the walls or holes in the ceiling as far as I can see. And we've drawn the drapes across the windows! And..."

"I'm on fire," someone interrupted. It was Bart who panicked. Hopping from one end of the room to the other, he chanted, "I'm on fire! I'm on fire!" Horrified, the others froze.

"What's going on?" Pete demanded. Pointing an accusing finger at Phil, he growled at Bart, "You've been listening to him too long. Calm down! We've got to get down to work, elect a chair, a recording secretary, and establish an agenda. And we can't do this overnight, or even the next few nights. We'll need to facilitate finding a facilitator for this process." Slowly he repeated his earlier warning, "We've got to take this one step at a time—*one* step at a time in an orderly fashion...."

No sooner had he said "orderly fashion" than a breeze, stronger and colder than the first, swept through the room causing everyone's tunics to billow like colorful parachutes. Bare legs and bottoms blossomed instantly amid cries of "Wowee! Wowee! It's freezing! Where's the wind coming from?"

Teeth chattering, some complained of the breeze while others cried, "Fire! Fire! Fire! I'm on fire!"

Still others chanted, "Freezing below and fire above! Freezing below and fire above!"

"Get hold of yourselves! Easy now!" Pete scurried from person to person to prevent more panic from spreading. Scrambling atop the table, he raised both hands and whispered, "Shhh! Shhh! Shhh! Control yourselves! What's gonna happen if we're carried away with all this nonsense about fire and wind? I'll tell you! If we're not careful, *careful*, I say, we'll end up throwing open the doors, the windows, and crawling out on the roof. Do you want to do something crazy like that? Huh?"

"But Pete," Phil pleaded, "Do we have any choice? More and more of us are having trouble wondering how long we can hide here."

"Hide?" Pete's eyes opened wide. "Did you say 'hide'?"

"I mean 'work' here," Phil quickly corrected himself.

"But you really meant 'hide' didn't you?"

"Pete, my head's not clear anymore. All I know is we seem to be avoiding whatever is outside those windows and doors."

Beads of perspiration gathered on Pete's forehead. "Are you saying, I say, are you saying we're staying here because we're afraid?" Pete asked defensively. Waving his hands wildly, he blurted, "If I'm afraid, then may my head be as hot as yours. Hot! Hot! Hot!" he cried. But each time he said the word "hot" his bald head turned a deeper shade of red. "Oh my god! My head's on fire!" he cried. Then a loud woooshhhh filled the whole room.

Once more their tunics ballooned, but this time the disciples were blown this way and that as they careened into chairs, walls, and one another. And with one voice they cried, "We're all on fire. We can't sit still. The wind's driving us, playing with us, making us restless. No more excuses! No more excuses! We've got to go. We've work to do and it isn't here. We've got people to see and places to go! We got to preach the good news! Jesus is alive! Jesus is alive!"

His face glowing joyfully, Pete chimed in, "I'm on fire. I'm on fire. And the wind is at my back. I can't stay here anymore. Unbar the doors! Throw open the windows!"

The order given, all the disciples rushed the doors and windows, flew them open to the world as the bright light streamed in and filled the room. Skipping onto the rooftop, they boldly proclaimed to passersby, "Do we have news for you! Good news! Hot news! Saving news! Watch out! We're on our way!"

Foreigners and native alike thought the disciples were drunk even though it was only nine in the morning. "Oh yes! Oh yes!" Pete cried. "We're drunk, but not with booze! We're drunk with the Spirit—with the wind and the fire! And we're on our way! We're on the way!"

The good news was about to spread like wildfire!

Fired Up With The Good News
Reflection

Jesus sought to counter the attitude that being ritually clean automatically made one acceptable in God's eyes. The quest for holiness through being morally and physically integral needed to be balanced with the practice of compassion toward all persons. Jesus wanted his disciples to do as he did. However his absence revealed his disciples' feeling lost, and incapable of bringing Jesus' good news to others. Only when they were moved by the Spirit to admit they were fearful and hiding could they find themselves inspired to go forth and preach that news. In the words of Amazing Grace, "I once was lost and now I'm found."

In the Acts of the Apostles we read that when the apostles left the upper room they preached to "Parthians, Medes, Elamites, and residents of Mesopotamia, Judea and Cappadocia, Pontus and Asia, Phrygia and Pamphylia, Egypt and the parts of Libya belonging to Cyrene, and visitors from Rome, both Jews and proselytes, Cretans and Arabs..." (Acts 2:9-11).

What Fired Up With The Good News emphasizes is the natural fear which preaching Jesus' message might entail. Anyone who preaches or is called upon to preach truth to power, might think of reasons for procrastinating since preaching truth to power could mean being silenced, or losing one's job, or one's life. What finally compels one to preach the truth might not be like the drama described either in Acts or in this story. But the same Spirit of God is at work enabling one to lose the self, and find a self empowered by the Spirit to throw open windows, and preach the Word until it spreads like wildfire. Amazing Grace!

≫ EPILOGUE ≪

FINDING THE BODY OF CHRIST

In three stories of this volume (Saving Need, Broken Promise, and Fired Up With the Good News), each story is about Jesus' disciples searching for Jesus who is no longer available as he had been prior to his death. Finally when he does show himself he appears in unexpected ways, only to leave his disciples once more. Certainly they must have wondered where they would find Jesus again. The question we might ask ourselves is where are we to find the body of Christ?

Where can we find the body of Christ among all the other bodies in this world? Among the many bodies are the nobodies, or the losers, the lost and the least? Is this where we are to find the body of Christ? It isn't very easy to find the nobodies. These are the folks who have fallen through the cracks or seem to be invisible. We see through them, around them, above them but we do not see them. We avert our eyes, look the other way and pretend they aren't there. They are the homeless ones, these nobodies. They are the elderly hidden away in nursing homes, hidden perhaps so as not to remind us of our own fear of being nobodies. They are the folks imprisoned in our ghettos—fearful of being killed by random bullets. Sometimes they are also us, e.g., at a party where everybody knows everybody else except us as we stand in a corner of the room by ourselves. Yes, these are the nobodies. Is this where we can find the body of Christ? Well if they remain nobodies, people we see through, around, and above, and we see them only as nobodies, then we won't find the body of Christ here.

Maybe we can find the body of Christ in the anybodies of this world. They're more noticeable. Anybodies are known and prized for what they do. And we're all anybodies to some extent. Teachers, waiters, secretaries, actors, dentists, CEOs, etc. Anybodies can be famous or little known. Their value is in what they do. Anybodies, of course, are replaceable. So you're good at pulling teeth. When you leave the scene, there's another dentist in the wings waiting to take your place. So you're a great pencil sharpener. Here today, gone tomorrow! Anybodies are all over the place and all replaceable—some more difficult to replace than others—but all replaceable. Is this where we find the body of Christ? Well if the anybodies remain just anybodies to us, people who do things, then we won't find the body of Christ here.

Perhaps we can find Christ's body in the somebodies of the world. Just maybe we can find them here. Somebodies are unique and irreplaceable to those who love them. They mean something over and above an anybody to a lover, a friend, a mother, a husband, etc. When they are gone we grieve their loss. We might not even survive very long without that somebody who is gone. But as is the case with nobodies and anybodies, if somebodies are no more than somebodies, then unfortunately we won't find the body of Christ here either.

So if nobodies are just nobodies and nothing more, where is Christ's body?
And if anybodies are just anybodies and nothing more, then where is Christ's body?
And if somebodies are just somebodies and nothing more, then where is Christ's body?

But what if there's more to the nobodies, the anybodies and the somebodies than meets the eye? Have you ever heard the expression, "You're something else?" You're something else! There are those moments when we can look in the eyes of nobodies, anybodies and somebodies and marvel, "You're something else!" What's this something else that evokes our wonder, our awe, our reverence? What's this something else that tells us more than meets the eye in people whom we had seen as only nobodies, or only anybodies, or only somebodies?

It's in this "something else" that we might have found what we are looking for. Here in this person, this woman rocking in her rocking chair, here in this man tending his wife afflicted with Alzheimer's, here in the men and women tending those with AIDS as well as those with AIDS, here in those who assist dead men and women walking on death row...here when we whisper, cry or marvel, "You're something else," ...here we find the body of Christ! Some people are especially good at being able to see something else in someone else. The Dorothy Days, the Martin Luther Kings, the Mother Teresas—all people who look after others and see something else—Christ's body!

Some of us might be thinking we've really missed the most obvious place to find the body of Christ. Day after day, year after year, during the liturgy in the name of Jesus we hear uttered the words over the wafer of bread, "This is my Body" and over the wine, "This is my Blood!" And at communion how many times do the Eucharistic ministers say, "The Body of Christ?"

Yes, this is true. We do say this over and over. But what is also true is that we shall never see something else in this wafer or this wine until and unless we are ready to see something else, something more in the nobodies, the anybodies and the somebodies we come across. Nor shall we be able to celebrate the liturgy properly unless in our coming together we gradually become aware in our presence to one another that there is something else going on here, there is something else in each of us—God's life, God's blood coursing through our veins.

Do we realize—each of us—that when we

receive the body of Christ from the minister of the Eucharist that it is Christ receiving Christ. Christ is given to Christ to those who can see something else going on.

    Our spiritual journey is or ought to be a deepening realization of this something else in all of us. Some of us might feel like nobodies at times, anybodies at other times, and sometimes somebodies, but if we are truly seeking the body of Christ we shall do so if, eyes widened in amazement, we discover Christ's body whenever we cry, "You are something else." For in that something else is the body which binds all of us together—it is the body of Christ.